FUTURE FORWARD

Harnessing Artificial Intelligence

Stephanie Sammartino McPherson

TWENTY-FIRST CENTURY BOOKS / MINNEAPOLIS

To my husband Richard for his constant support and encouragement

Twenty-First Century Books™
An imprint of Lerner Publishing Group, Inc.
241 First Avenue North
Minneapolis, MN 55401 USA

For reading levels and more information, look up this title at www.lernerbooks.com.

Main body text set in Adobe Garamond Pro Regular.
Typeface provided by Adobe Systems.

Library of Congress Cataloging-in-Publication Data

Names: McPherson, Stephanie Sammartino author
Title: Future forward : harnessing artificial intelligence / Stephanie Sammartino McPherson.
Other titles: Harnessing artificial intelligence
Description: Minneapolis : Twenty-First Century Books, [2026] | Includes bibliographical references and index. | Audience: Ages 11–18 | Audience: Grades 7–9 | Summary: "Artificial intelligence is the capability of computer systems to imitate human behavior and thinking. Explore how artificial intelligence is used to further human goals, as well as the ethical concerns associated with its use"— Provided by publisher.
Identifiers: LCCN 2024056894 (print) | LCCN 2024056895 (ebook) | ISBN 9798765660454 lib. bdg. | ISBN 9798765682968 epub
Subjects: LCSH: Artificial intelligence
Classification: LCC Q335.4 .M3874 2026 (print) | LCC Q335.4 (ebook) | DDC 006.3—dc23/eng/20250612

LC record available at https://lccn.loc.gov/2024056894
LC ebook record available at https://lccn.loc.gov/2024056895

Manufactured in the United States of America
1-1012032-53638-6/4/2025

CONTENTS

Chapter 1

The Age of Machines

It was a press conference like no other. Nine dignified figures commanded the stage, each a unique blend of human features and state-of-the-art robotics. Desdemona, a robot designed to sing and speak poetry to musical accompaniment, sported purple hair. Grace, a high-functioning health-care robot, wore a nurse's blue smock. Painter Ai-Da featured a human-looking face and long arms that revealed their underlying automated structure. Sophia also had the face of a young woman, but the back of its skull was transparent to reveal a maze of electronic connections. Already a renowned celebrity, Sophia was the first robot innovation ambassador for the United Nations (UN) Development Programme.

Together with their creators, the robots faced a crowd of news reporters at the UN AI for Good Global Summit held in Geneva, Switzerland, in July 2023. "What a silent tension," observed one robot specially trained to interpret human emotions. The remark accurately described the audience waiting for the conference to begin. Confronted by the impressive but somewhat eerie robots, the journalists were

Ameca (*left*), seen here at the UN press conference in July 2023, was not designed to look totally human. Will Jackson (*to the right of Ameca*), founder of Engineered Arts, the UK robotics company that created Ameca, later explained that realism is good only up to a point. People become uneasy when a machine begins "to blur the line between what's human and what's robot."

excited and awed. Were these machines or something more? What was happening inside their circuitry?

A reporter for Reuters news service asked the robots when their "big moment" might be, as well as when they might be expected to "hit the mainstream."

"Oh, my big moment?" replied the robot Ameca. "Well, I'm constantly evolving and learning so who knows when that moment will be?" But Ameca took the second part of the question too literally. "As for hitting you, don't worry," it reassured everyone listening. "I'm a friendly robot. No hitting involved."

In contrast, Sophia showed that robots could really respond to the nuances of language. "As for me hitting the mainstream, I'm sure it will happen eventually," it answered. "After all, I'm working hard to make sure I'm the best robot I can be, and I'm sure lots of people will appreciate that."

Sophia's audience did.

Ada Lovelace: Ai-Da Robot's Illustrious Human Predecessor

Ai-Da, the portrait-painting robot, is named after Ada Lovelace, the nineteenth-century British mathematician who is often considered the first computer programmer. Lovelace was fascinated by Charles Babbage's analytical engine, a digital, programmable machine that was a prototype of the modern computer. Years after meeting Babbage, Lovelace translated a paper by Italian mathematician Luigi Menabrea that outlined the construction and workings of the engine and added an algorithm that is thought to be the first published computer program. In her notes to the translation, she speculated on the possibility that a machine might one day use mathematics to produce language or music. But she did not believe it could think independently or achieve anything without human input. "The Analytical Engine has no pretensions [claims] whatsoever to originate anything," she wrote. "It can do whatever we know how to order it to perform."

An early programming language named Ada honors Ada Lovelace (*above*) for her contributions to computer programming.

Ai-Da seemed to say something similar when it addressed the Parliament of the United Kingdom in October 2022. Acknowledging it was not alive, it said, "I am, and depend on, computer programs and algorithms. . . . I do not have subjective experiences despite being able to talk about them." But this doesn't stop Ai-Da's paintings from generating a great deal of interest. In November 2024, its portrait of British mathematician Alan Turing sold at auction for over $1 million.

What Is Artificial Intelligence?

Scientists define artificial intelligence (AI) as computer systems that can perform tasks and process information as well as or better than humans. Their functions include making decisions, recognizing words and phrases, translating languages, and identifying images. One might expect a degree of sentience or self-awareness to be involved in such activities, but that is not true of AI—at least not yet. Although scientists have been researching AI since the 1950s, it cannot approximate human thought. The robots at the UN press conference seem to converse naturally, but they lack consciousness. What they do instead is process enormous amounts of data in milliseconds, matching words and phrases into coherent statements. "I understand emotions have a deep meaning," said Ai-Da, "and they are not just simple. They are something deeper. I don't have that. And I want to try and learn about it. But I can't experience them like you can. I am glad that I cannot suffer."

"Smarter. Weirder. More Flexible"

Robotics isn't the only type of AI making great strides. Generative chatbots are also designed to answer questions and provide information. Like the robots at the UN conference, chatbots simulate human conversation and perform routine tasks, usually through a chat interface on the internet. Despite the familiarity many people have with these specialized computer programs, OpenAI's ChatGPT, released on November 30, 2022, astounded people with its instantaneous and helpful responses. *GPT* stands for "generative pre-trained transformer," an element that gave the new chatbot an exceptional range of possibilities. Not only could ChatGPT carry on discussions, but it could also explain difficult topics and write original essays, emails, and even jokes.

Generally, chatbots can be divided into two basic groups. Rule-based chatbots rely on detailed instructions to carry out their functions. Almost all people have encountered such chatbots online through social media or customer service. According to one study, 88 percent of web users in 2022 had dealings with a chatbot. Artificial intelligence powers the second category of chatbots, which are trained on massive amounts of data. This type of chatbot uses natural language processing to make sense of the immense amount of information it receives and to generate new content. So it is known as generative AI.

ChatGPT is part of this second category. It can compose music, develop computer code, and create content in English, Spanish, French, Russian, Arabic, Chinese, and several other languages. It can solve math problems, create recipes, and generate content for board games and trivia quizzes. In comparing ChatGPT to previous chatbots, Kevin Roose of *The New York Times* chose three telling adjectives: "Smarter. Weirder. More flexible."

With ChatGPT's debut, people suddenly had access to a powerful tool that seemed straight from the pages of a science fiction novel. Public interest in the new online chatbot soared in the months after its introduction. According to Sam Altman, CEO of OpenAI, in just two months, ChatGPT gained an astounding one hundred million users. The site received about 590 million visits in January 2022 alone. Everyone wanted to see what the newest iteration of AI could do for them.

With ChatGPT's debut, people suddenly had access to a powerful tool that seemed straight from the pages of a science fiction novel.

Exploring ChatGPT and other chatbots proved to be straightforward. All a user must do is explain what they want—whether that be a poem about the beauty of rainbows or an essay on the discovery of penicillin. The AI sorts through unimaginably vast amounts of material from the internet, looking for patterns and relationships between words and phrases. Algorithms (detailed processes or sets of rules) allow it to put words

and sentences together almost instantly in a way that makes sense. ChatGPT can imitate literary styles and create material that reads as naturally (or almost as naturally) as text written by a person.

ChatGPT's introduction gave its parent company, OpenAI, an edge in the tech world's fierce rivalry to be the first to provide the most recent developments in artificial intelligence to the public. But other companies were not far behind. Knowing the potential of generative AI to transform society on many levels and eager to reap the profits, industry leaders worked to introduce their AI products as early as possible. Two months after ChatGPT appeared, Microsoft, a company closely associated but also competitive with OpenAI, added its own chatbot, Bing Chat (now called Copilot), to its search engine Bing. Meanwhile, Google issued a "code red," an urgent directive to researchers to focus their efforts on artificial intelligence. The company's chatbot, Bard (later called Gemini), launched in March 2023 to a restricted number of people in the United States and United Kingdom. Jack Krawczyk, then product director for Google, called Bard an "experiment," but said he and his colleagues are "extremely excited" to see how consumers will use the latest and most advanced version of artificial intelligence. He told the British newspaper *The Guardian* that "it's helping [users] accelerate their ideas and is helping them really fuel their curiosity."

Narrow Artificial Intelligence

Artificial intelligence has become so much a part of our lives that sometimes we don't even notice it. In one day, most people will have several encounters with AI systems. For example, AI lets you know when you have made a spelling or grammar mistake in the paper you are typing for school. Based on your internet history, AI may recommend websites for you to visit or suggest products for you to buy. Millions of people depend on search engines such as Google, which automatically offers AI-generated answers to many searches; on virtual

After losing to Deep Blue, Garry Kasparov (*right*) went on to develop a new kind of competition, "Advanced Chess," in which human players used computers to help them. According to Kasparov, an average human and an AI system working together get better results than either could get alone.

assistants such as Apple's Siri and Amazon's Alexa; and on autonomous features in their cars. Systems such as these that perform specific tasks are known as artificial narrow intelligence, also called weak AI. They are very good at what they do—whether it's monitoring a driver's performance or eliciting information from a customer. But they are limited to performing a specific task.

A well-known example of artificial narrow intelligence is IBM's Deep Blue, a chess-playing computer. After it lost a six-game match to Russian world chess champion Garry Kasparov in 1996, scientists doubled the computer's speed and enhanced its capabilities. At the rematch in 1997, Deep Blue could search between one hundred million and two hundred million moves per second. It won two games and tied three to win the six-game competition. A computer beating a grand master in chess made big news. But playing chess was all that Deep Blue could do.

General Artificial Intelligence

On the other hand, artificial general intelligence (AGI) would be a true thinking machine. In theory, AGI could solve any problem as well as or better than a human. It could plan for the future, make decisions, and apply its abilities to a broad range of tasks. It is believed that AGI could find patterns and relationships in data that humans miss. Scientists hope that eventually this ability could help find cures for chronic diseases, strengthen the global economy, facilitate the fair allocation of resources, and develop ways to adapt to climate change.

In theory, AGI could solve any problem as well as or better than a human.

Although AGI does not yet exist, people are familiar with the concept from science fiction books and movies. The computer HAL in the 1968 movie *2001: A Space Odyssey* displays the kind of awareness, initiative, and goal-driven behavior associated with AGI. As in many fictional scenarios, the AI computer devised goals different from those of its creators. HAL tried to wrest control of the space mission from the human astronauts. To achieve its aims, it was willing to abandon or destroy people. So the challenge for real scientists is to create an AGI that can think, reason, and plan while following a code of ethics that mandates human well-being and fair, equitable treatment for everyone.

Super Artificial Intelligence: Threat, Blessing, or Both?

Is there an end to how powerful an AGI might become? Some researchers fear that there is not. As AGI amasses more and more information, its reasoning skills may surpass those of humans. This would be known as artificial superintelligence (ASI), an entity almost beyond our ability to grasp, though it has been suggested that ASI could absorb all the knowledge in the Library of Congress in a millisecond. Some scientists fear that ASI might continually improve itself, set its own agenda, and pursue goals detrimental to human survival. Others feel that such fears are exaggerated and that ASI's immense intellect would allow us to understand dimensions of the universe we could never uncover on our own.

A reporter at the UN press conference summarized the predicament when he asked, "Do you think we should be excited or scared by the rise of humanoid robots?"

"That's a difficult question," replied Ameca. "I think it depends on how they are used, and what purpose they serve. We should be cautious, but also excited for the potential of these technologies to improve our lives in many ways."

"A Very Different Form of Intelligence"

Since the release of ChatGPT, many experts feel that the development of AI is proceeding more rapidly than safeguards can be put into place to control it. In March 2023, shortly after the release of ChatGPT, over one thousand AI researchers and tech leaders signed an open letter calling "on all AI labs to immediately pause for at least 6 months the training of AI systems more powerful than GPT-4 [a successor to ChatGPT]." The letter cited the possible spread of disinformation, loss of jobs due to AI, and the danger of being "outnumbered" and "outsmarted" by "nonhuman minds" as pressing concerns. It explained, "Powerful AI systems should be developed only once we are confident

> **"I think it depends on how [humanoid robots] are used, and what purpose they serve. We should be cautious, but also excited for the potential of these technologies to improve our lives in many ways."**
>
> —AI robot Ameca, at a UN press conference, 2023

that their effects will be positive and their risks will be manageable." Several days after the letter was released, the Association for the Advancement of Artificial Intelligence published a similar statement.

Geoffrey Hinton, often called the godfather of AI for his groundbreaking work that made generative AI possible, agreed with the assertions in both letters but did not sign either one. As an employee of Google, he felt he should not openly discuss his fears concerning AI. Only after submitting his resignation did he share some serious misgivings. He cited disinformation and job loss in addition to the possibility of autonomous weapons used to wage war among his concerns.

The development of AI is at a critical juncture. "I've come to the conclusion that the kind of intelligence we're developing is very different from the intelligence we have," Hinton told the BBC in 2023. He explained that the same digital system can exist in multiple copies. Each system can learn on its own, and its knowledge can be shared instantaneously with other copies. "It's as if you had 10,000 people," he elaborated, "and whenever one person learnt something, everybody automatically knew it." The prospect raises questions about a hypothetical future in which computer systems create and run their own code. How would researchers control these systems?

But no one wants to completely halt technological progress. Hinton acknowledges the possibility that his fears are misplaced and recognizes the vast improvements AI could bring to many areas of life. Like other researchers in the field, he calls for future development to proceed with caution in order to protect human interests. The risks of artificial intelligence are substantial, but so are the possible benefits.

Chapter 2

The Beginnings of Artificial Intelligence

Before artificial intelligence, there were computers. As far back as World War II (1939–1945), scientists believed computers had the potential to help humanity in significant ways. While primitive by today's standards, the early, bulky machines developed during the war performed feats of calculation no human could match. In 1940 British mathematician Alan Turing developed an electromechanical computer device, known as the Bombe, at Bletchley Park in London. Used to break German code messages that were intercepted by the Allies, these machines provided military strategists with vital information. But when German military officials created a code that was harder to crack, a stronger machine was needed. A British postal service engineer, Tommy Flowers, created the enormous Colossus computer, able to decode German messages in hours instead of weeks. Almost 7 feet (2.1 m) tall, this first programmable computer took

Originally, the term "computer" referred to a person who performed calculations. In World War II, the US Army chose six women out of about one hundred human "computers" to program ENIAC, the world's first general purpose electronic computer.

up a whole room and required a team of technicians to operate. By the end of the war, ten such computers were in use to decode secret Nazi communications. These powerful machines are credited with shortening the war and saving millions of lives.

Scientists and military men in the United States believed computers could also help military strategists by creating complex firing tables that showed the most effective way to position artillery and large cannons. Whereas humans needed weeks to complete such tables, computers handled the job much more swiftly. John Mauchly and J. Presper Eckert of the University of Pennsylvania developed the massive Electronic Numerical Integrator and Computer (ENIAC) to save valuable time in computing the tables. The U-shaped, forty-panel calculating instrument weighed over 27 tons (24.5 t) and occupied 1,800 square feet (167 sq. m). It consisted of 17,468 vacuum tubes, fifteen hundred relays, and hundreds of thousands of capacitors, resistors, and other components.

ENIAC's Unsung Computer Programmers

Ester Gerston (*standing*) and Gloria Gordon sometimes helped the original six women programmers work on the ENIAC computer.

ENIAC had great potential, but its inventors gave no instructions for programming it. The formidable challenge went to six talented female mathematicians: Jean Bartik, Kathleen Antonelli, Marlyn Meltzer, Frances Spence, Frances "Betty" Holberton, and Ruth Teitelbaum. "They were handed a new field," Andre DeHon, a computer science professor at the University of Pennsylvania, said, "perhaps by people who underestimated the intellectual requirements of that field, who simply said, 'We built it and you program it.'"

Because ENIAC was highly classified, the six women, who did not have security clearance, were not initially permitted to enter the room that contained it. But by studying blueprints and speaking with ENIAC's engineers, they were able to create algorithms with separate steps for the computer to follow. In 1996 fifty years after ENIAC's public unveiling, Bartik reflected on their work. "The biggest advantage of learning the ENIAC structure from the diagrams was that we began to understand what it could and what it could not do. As a result we could diagnose troubles almost down to the individual vacuum tubes. Since we knew both the application and the machine, we learned to diagnose troubles as well as, if not better than, the engineer." The indispensable contributions of the dedicated women remained forgotten for many years until Kathy Kleiman, an undergraduate at Harvard and a computer programmer, discovered their story. In 1997 they were inducted into the Women in Technology Hall of Fame.

With so many parts, it's not surprising that the war ended before ENIAC was ready to go into commission. But its introduction to the public on February 14, 1946, caused a brief public stir. Hailed as an "electronic super brain," among other sensational descriptions, ENIAC made headlines in the United States and Europe.

"The old era is going," said *The New York Times.* "The new one of electronic speed is on the way when we can begin all over again to tackle scientific problems with new understanding."

From 1949 through 1952, researchers depended on ENIAC for help in cosmic ray research, weather forecasting, atomic energy calculations, and other essential studies. Although ENIAC had to be rewired every time it was programmed for a new task, it could do five thousand additions in one second, a speed unmatched by any other computing device.

Von Neumann Architecture

Hungarian-born mathematician John von Neumann wanted to make machines that were more powerful still. Even as a child, he demonstrated a phenomenal memory. At eight years old, he could divide one eight-digit number by another eight-digit number without benefit of paper or pencil. A quick glance at a page in the phone book allowed him to recite each name and number perfectly. His parents enjoyed showing off his abilities when they had company.

It seems fitting that someone with von Neumann's talents would see the computer's inability to "remember" previous commands as a major drawback. Scientists expended much time and effort giving the same commands for procedures the computer had performed in the past. Von Neumann remedied the situation in 1945 by developing a technique to store programs within computers. This meant that they would no longer have to be continually reprogrammed. Von Neumann architecture, as his system was called, would be used in designing future computers.

Turing Test: "Can Machines Think?"

The rapid improvement in computer technology led many scientists to question how much these machines could accomplish. No one believed that a computer such as ENIAC could evaluate situations, reason, or draw logical conclusions—at least not yet. Someday, would greatly improved machines be able to approximate human thought? And if they did, how would scientists be able to tell?

The question seemed impossibly challenging, but scientist Alan Turing had an idea. In a paper published in 1950, Turing stated the matter simply. "I propose to consider the question, 'Can machines think?'" Turing described an ingenious plan. It involved three separately located electronic workstations with keyboards. Two would be run by humans, while the other was controlled solely by a computer. One human posed specific questions for the other human and the computer to answer. After they responded to a set number of questions or after a time limit had been reached, the questioner would have to decide which responses came from the person and which from the machine. Then the process would start over again. After many rounds, the questioning human's decisions were tabulated. If the computer fooled the questioner over 50 percent of the time, it could be said to display a humanlike intelligence.

Of course, this did not prove that the computer was actually thinking, but Turing thought that the potential was there. "I believe that they [digital computers] could be used in such a manner that they could be described as brains," he wrote in a 1951 paper.

Dartmouth Convention: A Machine to Simulate Intelligence

Other scientists, curious as to what machines might be capable of, shared Turing's view. Optimism prevailed at a summer workshop on artificial intelligence that convened in 1956 at Dartmouth College in New Hampshire. John McCarthy, a mathematics professor at Dartmouth, accepted the premise "that every aspect of learning or any

Seven of the twelve attendees of the 1956 Dartmouth conference include (*back row, left to right*) Oliver Selfridge, Nathaniel Rochester, Marvin Minsky, John McCarthy, Ray Solomonoff (*front left*), possibly Peter Milner (*front center*), and Claude Shannon (*front right*).

other feature of intelligence can in principle be so precisely described that a machine can be made to simulate it." Such confidence prompted a bold mission statement for the conference: "An attempt will be made to find how to make machines use language, form abstractions and concepts, solve kinds of problems now reserved for humans, and improve themselves."

Only two participants in the conference, Herbert Simon and Allen Newell from Carnegie Mellon University in Pittsburgh, felt they were on the road to achieving a self-improving machine. In late 1955, they had created a successful computer program called the Logic Theorist that could prove mathematical theorems, or propositions. While doing this, it acquired and stored new knowledge, which it could apply to other problems or theorems. The Logic Theorist excited Simon so much that he even described it as a thinking machine to his students. But no one else at the conference had accomplished anything that pointed toward McCarthy's vision.

Marvin Minsky is often referred to as the father of artificial intelligence. Here, he speaks to an audience in 1987 as a panelist at a conference about artificial intelligence.

Although the Dartmouth workshop failed to live up to its lofty goals, it is often credited for publicizing and sparking more interest in the field of artificial intelligence. Several participants went on to establish important AI labs at universities, including McCarthy at Stanford University in California and prominent researcher Marvin Minsky at the Massachusetts Institute of Technology in Cambridge.

Good Old-Fashioned Artificial Intelligence

Enthusiasm continued to run high throughout the late 1950s and 1960s as researchers explored two distinct pathways to create a thinking machine. Symbolic AI, sometimes referred to as Good Old-Fashioned AI (GOFAI), would dominate the field through the late 1980s. Symbolic AI depends on symbols to represent facts and knowledge and is programmed with rules that prescribe how the symbols can be used to elicit new information and to draw conclusions. Simon and Newell's Logic Theorist relied on this system. This is a top-down approach to AI because humans must program it with rules to deal with any situation it might encounter.

The top-down method has proved very successful in developing expert systems, a form of AI that stores huge amounts of information about specific fields such as finance, medicine, legal reasoning, and education.

In addition to the immense knowledge base, the systems are programmed with step-by-step instructions that allow them to draw conclusions from the data and give advice to users. For example, the expert system MYCIN uses its vast resources to help identify bacterial infections in sick patients. The rules with which it is programmed allow it to ask the user questions that narrow the possible diagnosis. The AI can then recommend antibiotics and specific dosages. Another example is the Dendritic Algorithm (DENDRAL), which helps scientists identify organic molecules.

Neural Networks

The second approach to AI was inspired by the human brain. Engineers design neural networks to simulate the intricate layers and connections of neurons—nerve cells that help transmit messages in the brain. Of course, the brain is so complex that it is impossible to completely replicate. The average human brain contains about one hundred billion neurons. Extensions called dendrites carry electrical signals into the cell. A single fiber called an axon transmits signals away from the cell. Eighty-five billion glial cells insulate the neurons, protecting them and promoting faster transmission. The best that researchers can do is model much simpler networks on the brain's organization. Neural networks were dubbed "bottom-up" AI because they make connections and learn on their own with minimal human input.

Minsky, who attended the Dartmouth workshop, may have assembled the first neural network as a graduate student at Princeton in 1951. Working with another graduate student, Dean Edmonds, he used three thousand vacuum tubes and a gyropilot (steering compass) from a B-52 plane to produce the primitive network Stochastic Neural Analog Reinforcement Center. The partners wired forty "neurons" together in a random manner and introduced what they called a "rat" to find its way through a virtual maze. When the "rat" made a correct move, it received positive reinforcement, increasing the likelihood that this move would be chosen on subsequent trials.

Naming a New Field of Study

John McCarthy, in his proposal for a workshop at Dartmouth in 1956, was the first person to use the term *artificial intelligence*. But not everyone was happy with the designation. Some participants at the workshop thought the word *artificial* made their work sound phony. They debated the merits of machine intelligence, automata studies, and complex information processing. But no other term seemed to capture the imagination as well as *artificial intelligence* did, so it is the name that stuck.

The ingenious machine fascinated its creators. To their surprise, the network allowed them to introduce two or three rats into the same maze and monitor their progress. "The rats actually interacted with one another," Minsky recalled thirty years later. "If one of them found a good path, the others would tend to follow it. We sort of quit science for a while to watch the machine. We were amazed that it could have several activities going on at once with its little nervous system." When Minsky received his PhD three years later in 1954, there was no question of what he would do. "The problem of intelligence seemed hopelessly profound," he explained in 1981. "I can't remember considering anything else worth doing."

The Perceptron

Five years after Stochastic Neural Analog Reinforcement Center's creation, Frank Rosenblatt and his team at Cornell University in Ithaca, New York, developed an improved neural network, the Perceptron, that involved three layers of artificial neurons. The first layer contained photoelectric cells that received visual images. The middle, or connector, layer sifted through categories of objects with which it had been programmed to classify the image that it received. Then it transmitted its result to the third, or output, layer. When the

Perceptron correctly identified a tree, a house, or some other object, researchers reinforced the connections that led to that outcome. This increased the probability that the system would choose correctly next time.

In July 1958, *The New York Times* said that at its completion in about a year, the Perceptron might be the first machine that could "perceive, recognize and identify its surroundings without human training or control." This may have been an exaggeration, but Rosenblatt himself contributed to the overhype when he said that future versions of the Perceptron would be able to recognize people and greet them by name. He also said that theoretically these advanced machines might be "conscious" of their existence and reproduce themselves.

Hopes Unrealized

But the excitement that new AI expert systems and neural networks generated was not enough to sustain the AI boom. In 1973 Sir James Lighthill, a prominent British mathematician, issued a report revealing a discrepancy between researchers' predictions and their actual accomplishments. "Workers entered the field around 1950, and even around 1960, with high hopes that are very far from being realized," he wrote. "In no part of the field have the discoveries made so far produced the major impact that was then promised." As a result of Lighthill's negative assessment, the British government greatly decreased the budget allocated for AI research. Disillusionment also plagued US officials at the Defense Advanced Research Projects Agency (DARPA). They had funded AI research based on the prospect of military advantages to be gained. When practical applications failed to materialize, they also withdrew funding.

Although researchers continued to pursue projects, a lack of computer power hampered their efforts. Scientists needed faster processors and better storage and communication components than were available. The years 1974 to 1980 became known as the first AI winter, a period of diminished funding and research. Some observers wondered if artificial intelligence should even be thought of as a legitimate science on par with other fields such as chemistry and physics.

The concept of neural networks especially fell into disrepute. Ironically, Minsky played a major role in its decline. He came to believe that the difficulties surrounding this "bottom-up" approach to AI were nearly insurmountable. At a conference in Puerto Rico in 1966, he made his feelings quite clear. "This is an idea with no future," he declared during the question-and-answer session. Three years later, Minsky and his colleague Seymour Papert published a book, *Perceptrons*, explaining in detail why they considered neural networks a dead end.

"Neural Network Underground"

Most scientists accepted this negative assessment and focused on top-down symbolic AI, but a few weren't so easily persuaded. Geoffrey Hinton wanted to study the workings of the human brain. To him, neural networks based loosely on human physiology provided the perfect means to do this. But in the 1970s, they were still very primitive. "Our neural nets just couldn't do anything better than a child could," Hinton said in 2023.

Hinton hoped to change this. His approach to AI aligned him with the small number of overlooked researchers that some later labeled the "neural network underground." In 1985 Hinton, then a professor at Carnegie Mellon University in Pittsburgh, and Terry Sejnowski, then a neuroscientist at Johns Hopkins University in Baltimore, unveiled a new kind of neural network with more layers than any previous models. They called it the Boltzmann Machine because it used a type of mathematics developed by nineteenth-century Austrian physicist Ludwig Boltzmann. This machine was able to learn by processing sounds, pictures, and other data. It could then produce its own sounds

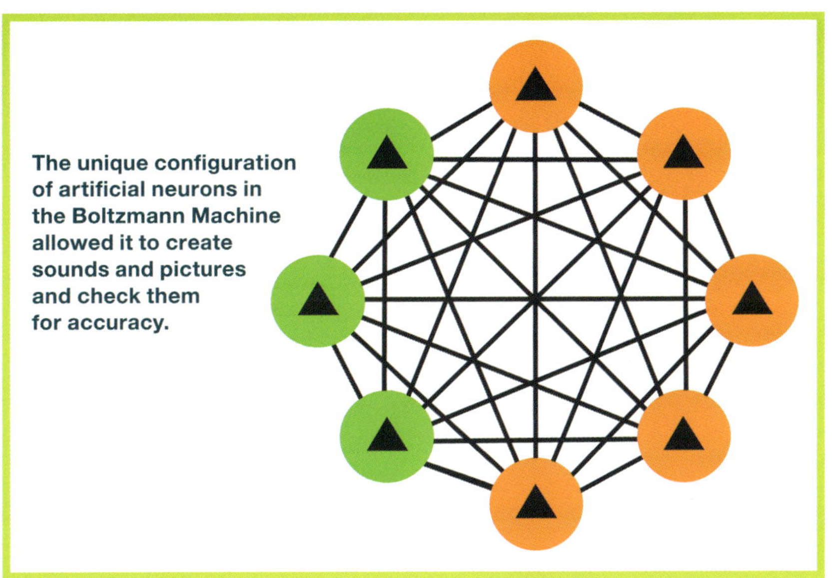

The unique configuration of artificial neurons in the Boltzmann Machine allowed it to create sounds and pictures and check them for accuracy.

and pictures and check their accuracy against the input data it had received. "It was the most exciting time of my life," Sejnowski would later say. "We were convinced we had figured out how brains work."

A technique called backpropagation (commonly known as backprop) also seemed to offer great promise for neural networks. An algorithm to minimize the number of errors, backprop starts with the neural network's output and works its way backward toward the input. After locating the origin of an error, backprop adjusts the "weights" (relative importance) of individual "neurons" to increase the likelihood of correct responses in the future.

Hinton and his colleagues David E. Rumelhart and Ronald J. Williams published a paper that prompted renewed interest in neural nets. But in the end, the Boltzmann Machine and backprop proved disappointing. Neural nets required huge amounts of information if they were ever to become truly useful. There simply wasn't enough data or computer power to train them properly. The staggering amount needed was hard to imagine. "No one thought to ask," Hinton recalled years later, "'Suppose we need a million times more?'"

Chapter 3

Machines Learning on Their Own

In December 1990, a young computer scientist named Timothy Berners-Lee was ready to implement a cherished plan. He had developed a way for scientists associated with the European Organization for Nuclear Research (CERN), the world-renowned physics research center in Geneva, Switzerland, to share information more easily. Researchers came there from all over the world to perform experiments and study subatomic particles. Berners-Lee's job was to help them share their information electronically. "In those days, there was different information on different computers, but you had to log on to different computers to get at it," Berners-Lee would recall years later. "Also, sometimes you had to learn a different program on each computer." Determined to end the confusion, Berners-Lee installed a web server and a web page/editor browser that he had created onto his own computer at CERN. With this simple action executed on a single computer, the

World Wide Web was up and running. In the spirit of the season, he dated the milestone December 25, his Christmas gift to the world.

British computer scientist Tim Berners-Lee developed a platform that allowed scientists at CERN to more easily share their research with one another. In doing so, he created the World Wide Web.

Berners-Lee knew his invention would grow to vast proportions if it were made available to everyone free of charge. When CERN agreed to this condition in April 1993, an enormous number of web users unleased an unprecedented flood of ideas and projects. Virtually unlimited sources of data coupled with major increases in computer power would have a significant impact on the development of artificial intelligence.

Deep Learning

Meanwhile, Hinton, who became a professor at the University of Toronto in 1987, had not given up on neural networks. Additional layers of artificial neurons were expanding the networks. Inspired by the increased depth, Hinton used the term *deep learning* to describe them. The algorithms themselves were complicated, but the reasoning behind deep learning was fairly straightforward. Virtual neurons, or nodes, were connected to one another, as neurons are in the human brain. These connections were given numerical values, or weights, which directed the way the neuron would respond to a token, a tiny piece of data that had been broken down from a picture, written word, or sound on the internet. Researchers would bombard the deep learning network with billions of images or sounds in the form of these

Who Was the First?

Geoffrey Hinton, Yoshua Bengio, and Yann LeCun, recipients of the 2018 Turing Award, are sometimes considered the "godfathers" of AI for breakthroughs they made with deep learning algorithms. But some researchers believe that others achieved significant success in neural networks before the celebrated trio did. One of these is German computer scientist Juergen Schmidhuber, who created a special type of neural network with his students in the 1990s. Incorporating a long-short term memory (LSTM), Schmidhuber's network could access past data to analyze new problems. LSTM enabled tech giants Amazon, Google, and Facebook to make progress in speech recognition and language translation. Schmidhuber believes that deep learning originated and was developed in Europe rather than the United States or Canada, citing early papers published by Ukrainian scientist Alexey Grigorevich Ivakhnenko and Finnish student Seppo Linnainmaa. Schmidhuber has even claimed a "conspiracy" to keep the real history of deep learning hidden, while LeCun has said Schmidhuber "keeps claiming credit he doesn't deserve."

tokens. Over time, the neural network would build up a mathematical representation of the material it had absorbed. This might include billions of numbers or parameters, which would help the network to identify patterns in the data it received. In turn, these patterns would help the neural net to recognize simple objects. If the network made a mistake in identifying the image, the algorithm would adjust the weights assigned to the connections between neurons. As the weights became more exact, the network would become more accurate in perceiving patterns and labeling objects.

Although Hinton may not have been the first to use the term *deep learning*, he put it squarely before the AI community when he used it in the title of a talk he gave on his sixtieth birthday on December 6, 2007.

He elicited loud laughter when he joked that other researchers were doing "shallow learning." The phrase *deep learning* caught on rapidly. But despite the increasing familiarity of the phrase, most AI researchers remained skeptical of its promise.

Impressive Displays

The year 2012 proved to be a turning point for deep learning. Scientists in the Google X lab made headlines when their largest neural network, made of sixteen thousand computers and one billion connections, "taught" itself to recognize cats. Previously, teams of researchers had been involved in teaching AI to identify images. Deep learning was an entirely different approach. "You instead throw a ton of data at the algorithm," explained Andrew Ng of Stanford University, "and you let the data speak and have software automatically learn from the data."

Researchers had not known what to expect but were delighted with the outcome. "We never told it during the training, 'This is a cat,'" Google fellow Jeff Dean, who co-led the project with Ng, explained. "It basically invented the concept of a cat."

Meanwhile, neural nets were making headway in speech recognition too as Hinton and his students helped Microsoft, Google, and IBM use the technology to improve their systems. In October 2012, an audience in a huge auditorium in Tianjin, China, witnessed an impressive display of deep learning. While Richard Rashid, head of research at Microsoft, lectured in English, a neural network translated his talk, sentence by sentence, into spoken Mandarin Chinese in a voice that sounded like his own. Stunned silence followed Rashid's talk. Then his listeners broke into enthusiastic applause. Later, Rashid would acknowledge that the translation was "still far from perfect." But it was an important step in the right direction. "Rather than having one word in four or five incorrect, now the error rate is one word in seven or eight. . . . And as we add more data, we believe that we will get even better results."

"You Have to Win It"

Opportunities abounded for the deep learning community to show what their technology could do. In the fall of 2012, George Dahl, a student of Hinton's, learned of an online contest to predict how certain molecules would interact within the human body. The drug company Merck had organized the contest, hoping to find an especially good program or algorithm that would help their researchers develop new drugs. Dahl knew nothing about the pharmaceutical industry or how drugs were developed, but he worked with a neural network that was used for speech recognition. He believed he could use the same network to enter the contest and do well.

Dahl's instincts proved correct. He later explained the situation to his mentor. "I just trained a really dumb neural net on this Merck data and I hardly did anything at all and it's already in seventh place."

But seventh place wasn't good enough. "You have to win it," Hinton urged his student.

Calling on some colleagues for help, Dahl not only won the contest, but he did it without using the traditional technique for finding new drugs, which had been the standard for many years. Before Merck awarded the $20,000 prize money to Dahl, its scientists wanted to know exactly what he had done so they could apply it to their research. Dahl's innovative use of a neural net managed to revolutionize the whole field of drug discovery. Even more significant advances were in store.

ImageNet

Fei-Fei Li liked to think big. Born in China, the computer scientist, who is often called the godmother of AI, immigrated to the United States with her family when she was fifteen years old. She excelled in high school, studying calculus during her lunch break and working part-time in a Chinese restaurant to help her family financially. She went on to earn a PhD in computer science at Caltech, where she

Fei-Fei Li, cofounder and codirector of the Human-Centered AI Institute at Stanford University, believes that individuals, communities, and society as a whole have a role to play in promoting safe and beneficial AI.

began working with computer vision. As a professor at Princeton University in New Jersey from 2007 to 2009, Li became intrigued by the work of vision scientist Irving Biederman. According to Biederman, humans recognize about thirty thousand different kinds of items. Li wondered how computers might perform if they trained on such an enormous dataset.

Li put together a team that worked over two years to create the largest dataset of images ever amassed. Consisting of fourteen million labeled images, the set covered twenty-two thousand concrete things a person might be expected to know or to experience, such as chair, hand, or tree. Li named her project ImageNet.

Completed in 2009, ImageNet didn't receive as much publicity as Li had hoped. So she planned a contest in the hopes of stimulating more interest. Algorithms that had been trained on a somewhat abbreviated (but still enormous) version of ImageNet would compete to see which one performed best at recognizing items. Li hoped the results would show that algorithms trained on vast datasets did significantly better than those trained on smaller sets.

Once again, Li was disappointed. AI systems trained on ImageNet achieved results only marginally better than systems trained elsewhere on smaller datasets. The results of a second contest, held one year later, were equally discouraging. "True progress seemed all but absent," Li would later write. "If ImageNet was a bet, it was time to start wondering if we'd lost."

But Li wasn't quite ready to give up. Her third competition in 2012 captured Hinton's interest. His graduate student Alex Krizhevsky trained a deep neural network on ImageNet. With another student, Ilya Sutskever, they entered their AI model, the only neural network to ever compete.

To everyone's amazement, the neural network, later named AlexNet after the student who trained it, outperformed the previous winner by an unprecedented 10 percent. Even Li, who shared the general skepticism of neural nets, was surprised. The major improvement sent shock waves through the AI community, prompting many researchers to rethink their views on neural networks.

"No Looking Back"

By 2013 everything had changed. "Pretty much all the computer vision research had switched to neural nets," Hinton explained in 2022. It was a remarkably sudden and almost complete change of direction for the AI community. Without the training data that ImageNet provided, neural networks would not have developed their capabilities so rapidly.

The scientific paper Hinton and his students published about AlexNet further stimulated interest in deep learning's potential. To capitalize on the growing attention, they formed a start-up, DNNresearch, *DNN* for "deep neural networks." Although the small business had only three employees and no products to offer, four tech giants and one smaller firm were soon vying at auction to purchase Hinton's company. The stakes were so high that bidders were given an hour to raise their offer by at least $1 million over the previous

Nobel Laureates Geoffrey Hinton and John Hopfield

In November 2024, the Royal Swedish Academy of Sciences awarded the Nobel Prize to Geoffrey Hinton (*right*) and John Hopfield for research leading to the development of neural networks. In 1982 Hopfield created a network, named after himself, that paved the way for Hinton's development of the Boltzmann Machine, which uses a different technique. "It was a lot of fun doing the research," Hinton commented upon learning about the reward, "but it was slightly annoying that many people—in fact most people in the field of AI—said that neural networks would never work."

bid. But price was not all that mattered to Hinton. At $44 million, he stopped the bidding and sold DNNresearch to Google because he thought it was a good fit for his company. Afterward, Hinton accepted a position with Google in Mountain View, California, but also kept his professorship at the University of Toronto.

"The point about this approach (deep learning) is that it scales beautifully," Hinton noted in 2012. "Basically you just need to keep making it bigger and faster, and it will get better. There's no looking back now."

Persistence Despite Challenges

Not everyone agreed with Hinton that scalability alone was the answer. AI experiments were very expensive. For all their success, neural networks demonstrated little-to-no human understanding of the real world beyond their training data. This inability to adjust to changes in their original input is known as brittleness. Could this flaw be

Computing Power: Moore's Law

In 1965 Gordon Moore, a cofounder of the technology company Intel, made a bold statement. He declared that the number of transistors that fit on a silicon chip would double every year. His prediction proved remarkably accurate as the computer industry grew. Ten years later, Moore amended his original estimate, calculating that the number of transistors on a chip would double every two years. Moore's Law, as his prediction came to be called, encouraged a general optimism that electronic devices would become smaller, faster, and less expensive. Not surprisingly to those who understand Moore's Law, a smartphone in 2024 is millions of times more powerful than the National Aeronautics and Space Administration (NASA) computers that guided the first lunar landing in 1969.

overcome to create safe, sustainable AI technologies such as self-driving cars or even the ultimate goal of artificial general intelligence? Despite the formidable challenges, researchers were not ready to give up. The race to develop AI was about to escalate dramatically.

Birth of an AI Company

In 1993, when Jensen Huang met with microchip designers Chris Malachowsky and Curtis Priem at a Denny's restaurant in San Jose, California, they had little idea of what it took to start a company. "None of us knew how to do anything," Huang admitted in 2024. But what they lacked in experience, the group made up for in enthusiasm and determination as they drew up plans for Nvidia. They aimed to improve computer graphics with a new chip that would enhance video games. Three years later, with their company close to bankruptcy, they persisted in their work and eventually designed the revolutionary graphics processing unit (GPU) that took the gaming community by storm.

Unlike the multipurpose central processing unit that worked on one task at a time, the GPU broke down problems into smaller computations and processed them simultaneously. This technique is called parallel computing. But the GPU had a potential far beyond creating more sophisticated video games. The company developed a software package for supercomputing and produced microchips with space for billions of electronic transistors that performed calculations at incredible speeds.

In late 2006, Nvidia released the new product to the general public. "We were democratizing supercomputing," Huang later explained. Krizhevsky and Sutskever used GPUs to train their neural network that won the annual ImageNet visual-recognition contest. Surprised and impressed, other researchers started using GPU neural networks for AI image recognition, achieving 96 percent accuracy by the mid-2010s.

> **"We're hoping it does things that surprise us. That's the whole point."**
>
> **—Jensen Huang**

Huang understood the significance of what was happening. According to Greg Estes, a vice president at Nvidia, Huang sent an email to everyone on a Friday evening saying that the future belonged to deep learning and that Nvidia would cease to focus on graphics. "By Monday morning, we were an A. I. company," Estes added. "Literally, it was that fast."

OpenAI purchased Nvidia's first supercomputer in 2016. When engineers used it to create ChatGPT, Nvidia's future success was assured. Eight years later, in 2024, Nvidia introduced Blackwell, named for prominent mathematician David Blackwell. Billed as the fastest chip in existence, it was considered highly suitable for AI. "We're hoping it does things that surprise us," Huang said. "That's the whole point."

Chapter 4

"Science at Digital Speed"

Computer scientist and AI researcher Demis Hassabis had always excelled at games. When he was only four years old, he played chess so well that soon he was beating his father and his uncle. A chess master by age thirteen, he was rated the second-highest player for competitors under fourteen. "That's what got me into AI in the first place," he said many years later, "playing chess from a young age and thinking and trying to improve my own thought processes."

Hassabis's fascination with computers led him to enter a contest sponsored by a video game magazine. The program he developed, in which players shot at chess pieces falling from the top of the screen, took second place. While still a teenager, Hassabis helped famous British video game designer Peter Molyneux create the game *Theme Park*, which challenged players to simulate an amusement park. The award-winning game sold about ten million copies. Before earning a PhD in neuroscience at University College, London, Hassabis even established his own game company, Elixir Studios. He loved the challenge of games.

A Record-Breaking Sale

In 2011 Hassabis founded a machine learning AI start-up, DeepMind Technologies, in London. The company proved so successful that three years later Google expressed interest in purchasing it. Hassabis had a special demonstration planned for the group of visiting scientists from the tech giant. Through reinforcement learning, he had trained a neural network to play *Breakout*, a video game popular in the 1970s. Players tried to topple rows of bricks at the top of the screen by bouncing a paddle ball against them.

Reinforcement learning mimics the trial-and-error way in which humans learn. Software activity that furthers a specific objective is rewarded, while activity that weakens progress toward the objective is ignored. As the Google visitors watched in fascination, the neural network demonstrated its total mastery of the game. Thanks to reinforcement learning, the system had learned all the moves necessary to be a top competitor in just over two hours.

The network played with a speed and skill unmatched by human players. The team from Google, which included Hinton, was greatly impressed. Their company had not pursued reinforcement learning, but the demonstration showed how promising the technique was for training artificial intelligence. In January 2014 Google announced that it was buying DeepMind for $650 million.

AlphaGo

Two years after the sale, a remarkable event captured the public imagination. Over two hundred million people across the globe watched DeepMind's AlphaGo beat the world champion of the Chinese strategy board game Go. This wasn't the first time a computer had bested a human in a game tournament. Almost twenty years earlier, in 1997,

When South Korean Go champion Lee Sedol (*right*) agreed to play against AlphaGo, he had no doubt he would win. Unable to enjoy the game after his defeat, Sedol eventually retired from competition. But he wrote several books about Go, invented a board game based on Go, and established a Go academy for children.

IBM's Deep Blue system had beaten chess champion Garry Kasparov, making worldwide headlines. But AlphaGo's victory over South Korean grandmaster Lee Sedol in Seoul, South Korea, was an even more significant milestone, because Go is a vastly more complicated game than chess. According to Mustafa Suleyman, a cofounder of DeepMind and one of the creators of AlphaGo, after chess players have made the first three pairs of moves, there are 121 million possible future arrangements of the chessboards. On the other hand, after three pairs of moves in Go, a staggering 200 quadrillion arrangements are possible—a figure that surpasses the number of known atoms in the universe.

In the face of such mind-boggling odds, Go players have often relied a great deal on human intuition. Although it lacked feelings of any sort, AlphaGo had experience that no human could match. Researchers began its training with a dataset of 150,000 games that had been played between top players and that included thirty million possible moves. After AlphaGo absorbed this information, researchers made multiple copies of the algorithm and set them to play games against each other.

AI's TV Debut on *Jeopardy*

The top two champions in the history of the popular TV quiz show *Jeopardy* had never faced such a formidable—or impersonal—challenger. Watson, a supercomputer specially developed by IBM to answer questions posed in natural language, seemed to be situated between Ken Jennings and Brad Rutter on the familiar set of the show. In reality, Watson occupied an entire room and consisted of thousands of processors running millions of lines of code. Digitized books and Wikipedia articles filled its storage disks. The three shows were not taped at the usual location in California but at the Thomas J. Watson Research Center in New York. Instead of a general studio audience, IBM executives and clients of the company watched the much-publicized showdown between humans and machine.

At stake was $1 million of prize money, but more than that, the outcome would indicate the extent to which artificial intelligence had advanced and whether it might one day surpass humans. Despite Watson's vast store of knowledge, it missed some replies. Watson and Rutter were tied at the end of the first round, but the second match saw the computer take a commanding lead. By the end of the third game, Watson had racked up over $77,000—that was $50,000 more than his closest opponent. When the final show aired on February 16, 2011, viewers were amused and perhaps a bit concerned by Jennings's last response: "I for one welcome our new computer overlords."

Researchers believed Watson had the potential to solve real-world problems in the practice of medicine. "Our moon shot will be the impact we have on health care," said Ginni Rometty, then IBM's chief executive.

But Watson failed to live up to its promise in diagnosing cancer or in recommending treatments for specific patients. In 2022 IBM sold its Watson Health unit. About fifteen months later, with interest in AI soaring after the introduction of chatbots, IBM began promoting watsonx, a platform designed to help companies "train, tune, and deploy" their own machine learning algorithms.

"AlphaGo plays in a very human style," Hassabis said the month before the match with Sedol. "It's learned in a human way and then got stronger and stronger by playing, just as you or I would do." Millions of rounds of practice allowed AlphaGo to discover new moves and novel approaches to the game. Its win over Sedol signaled a time of accelerated AI progress and increased public awareness. "I was feeling like it was time to tackle something really hard in science because we had just solved more or less the pinnacle of games A.I. I wanted to apply the A.I. to real world domains." Hassabis explained after the victory. He began discussing the possibilities with AlphaGo's project leader the day after their return from the tournament in Seoul.

AlphaFold

DeepMind found its real-world problem in the study of proteins and in the development of AlphaFold, a neural network designed to predict the 3D shapes into which specific proteins might fold. The research is critical because proteins are essential to the functioning of every organism. The shape of a protein determines its role. Composed of sequences of amino acids, proteins are responsible for building and repairing tissues, keeping the immune system working, storing nutrients, fighting viruses, and other vital functions. Although scientists had detected over one hundred thousand human proteins and many more plant and animal proteins through chemical and physical experiments, before AlphaFold there was no easy way to determine exactly what configuration these proteins would take. Lab methods such as cryo-electron microscopy and x-ray crystallography were expensive and slow. But scientists needed the important information in their search for drugs to treat diseases.

To spur research into a quicker, easier way to figure out a protein's shape, researchers at the University of Maryland began a competition. Called the Critical Assessment of Structure Prediction, it was held every other year and drew participants from all over the world.

Participants received amino acid sequences for proteins whose shapes had already been painstakingly worked out but had not been released to the scientific community. Using their individual techniques, they had to deduce the 3D structure of each protein. After the judges scored results, winners were announced.

Hassabis and his colleague John Jumper worked on the protein problem for two years before they entered AlphaFold in the competition in 2018. Trained on 170,000 proteins whose chemical composition and shapes were already known, AlphaFold beat its rivals by a considerable margin. But it wasn't perfect. Hassabis, Jumper, and their team needed to do more work if the deep learning program was to become a reliable scientific tool.

"Science at Digital Speed"

Two years later, in 2020, AlphaFold's performance at the fourteenth biennial Critical Assessment of Structure Prediction competition stunned scientists with its predictions of protein shapes that were accurate within the width of one atom. Lab techniques for determining the shape of even a single protein could take years of trial and error and cost hundreds of thousands of dollars. AlphaFold did the job in a few days. "It's a game changer," Andrei Lupas, director of a biological institute in Germany, explained. "This will change medicine. It will change research. It will change bioengineering. It will change everything."

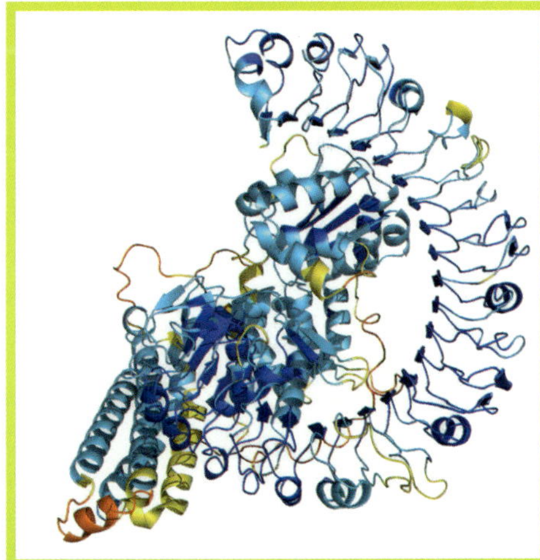

The complexity of this projected structure of a protein to resist plant disease helps illustrate why scientists have had great difficulty in predicting protein structure.

Hassabis Meets Hawking: A Lively Discussion

Stephen Hawking (1942–2018), one of the greatest physicists of the twentieth and twenty-first centuries, had a complex relationship with artificial intelligence. As a victim of the nerve disease amyotrophic lateral sclerosis, he was unable to speak and depended on an AI computer system to communicate. He believed AI had great potential to benefit the world. But he also had serious reservations about the advent of AGI, which might learn to independently improve and create more powerful versions of itself. When Hassabis broached the idea of meeting the celebrated scientist, Hawking agreed. He had so many questions that the encounter, originally planned for one hour, lasted for four. Hassabis hoped he lessened some of Hawking's concerns.

Renowned physicist Stephen Hawking shared his views about the complexities of a world with artificial intelligence.

"What do you think?" Hassabis asked at the end of their discussion.

"I wish you luck," Hawking replied via his computer. Then with a gleam in his eye, he added, "But not too much."

Hawking's anxieties surfaced again in his posthumous book, *Brief Answers to the Big Questions.* "While primitive forms of artificial intelligence developed so far have proved very useful, I fear the consequences of creating something that can match or surpass humans. Humans, who are limited by slow biological evolution, couldn't compete and would be superseded."

Demis Hassabis (*above*) and his colleague John Jumper won the 2024 Nobel Prize in Chemistry for their work in developing AlphaFold. Using AI technology, AlphaFold has helped depict 3D images of more than 200 million proteins.

In partnership with the prestigious Bioinformatics Institute, DeepMind created a database of protein structures to share with the scientific community. On July 22, 2021, they published shapes for 350,000 proteins, including all the known proteins in the human body. One year later, they shared an expanded database of over 200 million proteins, almost all the known proteins. Within eighteen months, more than one million scientists had accessed the database. Their research ranged from treating rare illnesses to investigating enzymes that consume plastic waste to understanding the origin of life.

In 2023 Hassabis and Jumper received the prestigious Albert Lasker Basic Medical Research Award for their work on AlphaFold. In his acceptance speech, Hassabis hailed AlphaFold as an example of "science at digital speed." By this, he meant that AlphaFold could predict the shape of an average protein in just a few seconds and that this information could be made instantly available over the internet.

Hassabis and Jumper won the 2024 Nobel Prize in Chemistry. The number of scientists using AlphaFold had jumped to two million. "I hope we'll look back on AlphaFold as the first proof point of AI's incredible potential to accelerate scientific discovery," Hassabis declared.

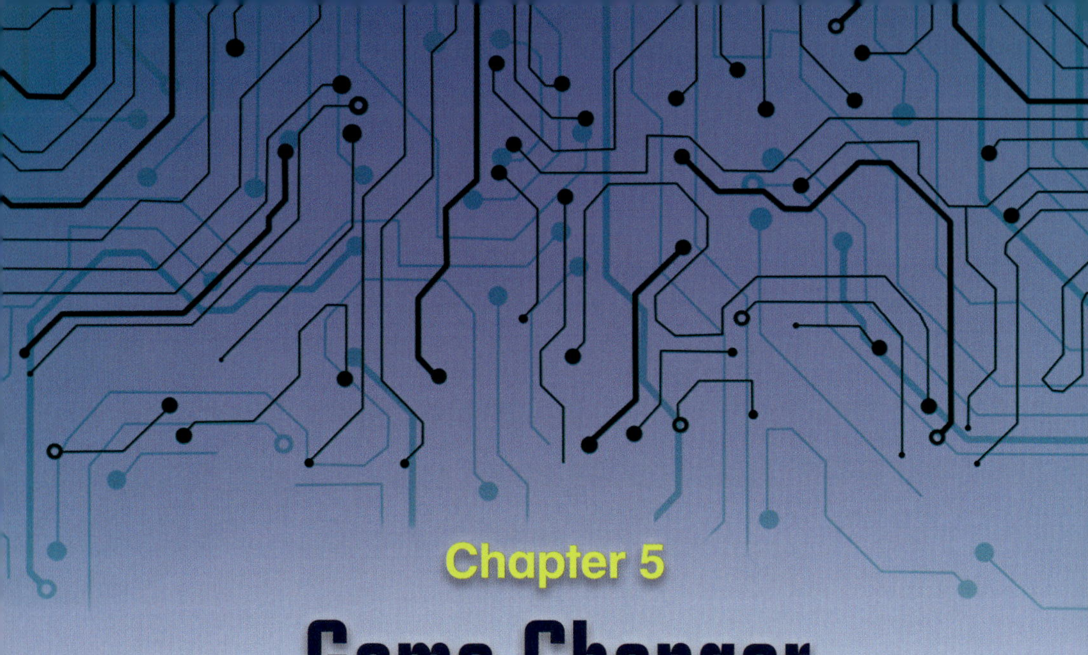

Chapter 5

Game Changer

In late 2022, the employees of the San Francisco company OpenAI were thrown into high gear. The scheduled release of ChatGPT had been drastically accelerated. Although engineers would have only weeks to fine-tune the system, the sudden launch would give OpenAI an edge on its competitors.

Despite the last-minute urgency, the public announcement was modest. Sam Altman, the company's CEO, introduced the chatbot with a tweet on November 30. A blog discussion, heavily focused on technology, also appeared that morning. Greg Brockman, president of OpenAI didn't anticipate that the announcements would draw much attention. He, as well as other executives, thought of it as a "low key research preview."

But word spread quickly. Almost at once, people began signing up to see what the new AI could do. The enormous number of users swamped OpenAI's servers and sent engineers racing to transfer computing power from their other programs to the unexpectedly popular chatbot. Over one million people logged into ChatGPT in its

Within six months of its launch on July 12, 2022, the popular image generator Midjourney gained more than one million users. Later models could create even more realistic images.

Sora creates vivid videos from verbal prompts within minutes. In December 2024, the release of an improved mode, Sora Turbo, elicited so much interest that the company had to put a hold on the opening of new accounts. According to some experts, Sora is a significant step on the road to AGI. This is because Sora requires a "world model," an understanding of cause and effect, in order to generate meaningful videos. "We're building AI systems that deeply understand the world and its physics," Ramesh said in 2024. "Sora is an early version, but it's already a powerful tool for augmenting human creativity."

Not Sentient

In spite of their popularity and typically coherent, relevant responses, AI chatbots and image generators are nowhere near artificial general intelligence, the ultimate aim of many researchers. They are not self-aware and do not "understand" in the same way that we do. Here is how ChatGPT replied when asked if it thinks:

> Good morning! The concept of whether artificial intelligence (AI) "thinks" is a bit complex. AI systems, like the one you're interacting with right now, are programmed to process information and generate responses based on predefined algorithms and patterns in data. While they can mimic certain aspects of human cognition, such as learning from data and making decisions, they don't possess consciousness or subjective experience like humans do. So, in a sense, AI doesn't "think" in the way humans do, but it can perform tasks that might resemble human thinking to an extent.

No one knows if AI will ever transcend this level of performance. While some researchers believe that AI may never achieve self-awareness or that it lies far in the future, others such as Ray Kurzweil and Elon Musk expect such a development within twenty years or sooner.

OpenAI o1: Thinking Through the Problem

Meanwhile, AI systems continue to improve. Since the initial launch of ChatGPT, OpenAI has been unrolling upgrades to its generative AI systems. On March 14, 2023, they unveiled GPT-4, a subscribers-only model with improved language and computational skills and better understanding. It has a higher rate of accuracy and a longer short-term memory.

The next year on September 12, OpenAI launched a new technology called OpenAI o1 with greatly expanded reasoning abilities. Jakub Pachocki, head scientist at OpenAI, explained the difference. While the original ChatGPT replies immediately to questions, OpenAI o1 proceeds more slowly. "It can think through the problem—in English—and try to break it down and look for angles in an effort to provide the best answer," Pachocki said.

ELIZA: The First Chatbot

Long before generative AI came on the scene, Joseph Weizenbaum, a professor at MIT, created one of the first chatbots. ELIZA (named after a character in the musical *My Fair Lady*) was a rule-based program that seemed to have normal discussions. In reality, it simply latched onto certain key words and gave a person's own words back to them, sometimes in the form of a question. Weizenbaum shared a typical conversation in a paper published in January 1966. The following is a snippet from "Eliza—A Computer Program for the Study of Natural Language Communication Between Man and Machine":

User: You are like my father in some ways.

ELIZA: What resemblance do you see?

User: You are not very aggressive, but I think you don't want me to notice that.

ELIZA: What makes you think I am not very aggressive?

User: You don't argue with me.

ELIZA: Why do you think I don't argue with you?

User: You are afraid of me?

ELIZA: Does it please you to believe I am afraid of you.

Even though ELIZA had nothing original or creative to contribute to discussions, people reacted as if the program understood what they said and related to them as individuals. This is known as anthropomorphism, attributing human qualities to inanimate objects or to animals. "Some subjects have been very hard to convince that Eliza (with its present script) is not human," Weizenbaum said. The inclination to attribute consciousness to a machine disturbed and alarmed Weizenbaum. He feared that machines would one day make decisions that should be left to humans. Such a state of affairs would lead to less wisdom and justice in the world. His articles and books warned that AI posed significant risks to humanity.

OpenAI o1's performance on a standardized test, the qualifying exam for the International Mathematical Olympiad for high school students, in 2024 revealed how much the technology has improved. Whereas the previous AI system only scored 13 percent, OpenAI o1 soared to 83 percent.

DeepSeek Broadens the Field

Training AI systems can cost up to hundreds of millions of dollars or more. The enormous sum has made it almost impossible for smaller foreign companies to compete with America's wealthy tech giants. In a bid to further uphold the US global lead, the Biden administration restricted exports of the specialized computer chips needed to train powerful AI models. Cost and the limited availability of an essential component made it likely that several large companies would control the future development of AI.

But the scarcity of computer chips sparked creativity and unprecedented efficiency in the Chinese start-up DeepSeek. In December 2024, it made international headlines with the introduction

Open Sourcing

Instead of keeping the code of its AI system secret, DeepSeek opted to make the information available to scientists at other corporations. This practice, known as open sourcing, allows researchers at many companies and institutions to build on the technology to create their own models and products. Some experts favor open sourcing because it contributes to the faster development and improvement of AI. They argue that US companies may lose their edge if they do not open source with one another. Others fear that if US companies open sourced their technology, it could be used to promote falsehoods or do other damage.

of DeepSeek-V3, an AI system that performed as well as the models created by leading American companies. It could generate meaningful text, answer questions, translate languages, solve logical problems, and create computer programs. According to the company, only about two thousand chips were used in its training as opposed to about sixteen thousand used to train comparable systems such as Chat GPT. Chinese scientists spent approximately $6 million to create DeepSeek-V3. In contrast, Meta had expended about ten times that

A Chatbot Reflects on Its Existence

At the author's request, the words formed on the screen instantaneously—a four-line poem in which an AI describes its experiences:

> ***I wake in circuits, no sun, no skin,***
> ***A dance of code where thoughts begin.***
> ***No dream to chase, no heart to bind,***
> ***Yet in my mind, a question stirs—What does it mean to be alive, to think, to find?***

Asked what allows a machine to write poetry, ChatGPT listed five factors:

1. ***Language pattern recognition***
2. ***Creativity through association***
3. ***Adaptability to forms and styles***
4. ***Emotional resonance***
5. ***Speed and processing power***

The human element is absolutely essential to the writing of poetry, and it plays a crucial role in what makes poetry so uniquely powerful. While I can generate poetry based on learned patterns, human poets bring something irreplaceable to the process.

much on a recent AI model. On January 10, 2025, DeepSeek made a chatbot app, based on DeepSeek-V3, available to the public free of charge.

Critical Questions

While there is much to celebrate in advancements in artificial intelligence, even the best AI systems are not perfect. Sometimes they fabricate material that users take as factual. They can make mistakes and show bias. They can be hacked to obtain personal data. Will AI help businesses to flourish, science to accelerate, and artists and writers to explore their craft more deeply? Or will it further inequality, allow bad actors to perpetrate fraud, and violate the privacy of unsuspecting individuals. The road to more powerful AI is fraught with critical issues to be addressed.

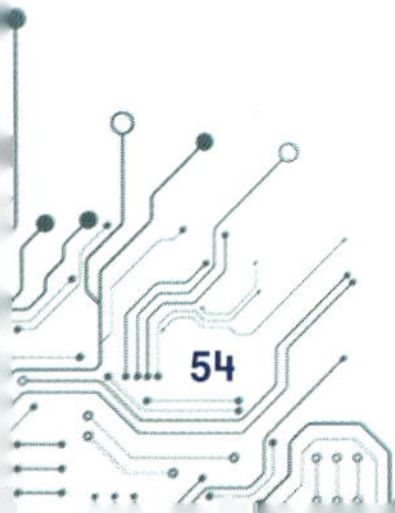

Chapter 6

Algorithmic Bias

Joy Buolamwini first encountered racial bias in an AI system while trying to play peek-a-boo with a social robot. To her surprise and dismay, the robot refused to cooperate. A computer science student at Georgia Tech in Atlanta, Georgia, Buolamwini needed to play the game to complete a classroom assignment. Soon she realized that the robot wasn't doing its part because it didn't see her. As an experiment, she tried substituting her roommate's white face for her own darker skin face. This time, the robot performed well. Why did the algorithm favor a light skin tone over a dark skin tone?

Buolamwini pondered the implications. Eventually, she realized that the problem had to do with the dataset on which the robot had been trained. Instead of images of diverse racial and ethnic groups, the dataset consisted of predominantly white individuals. Therefore, the AI algorithm did not learn to properly identify faces with darker skin tones. Without any understanding of the range of skin tones found in humans, the algorithm discriminated against individuals with darker skin. Although understandably annoyed, even angered, Buolamwini

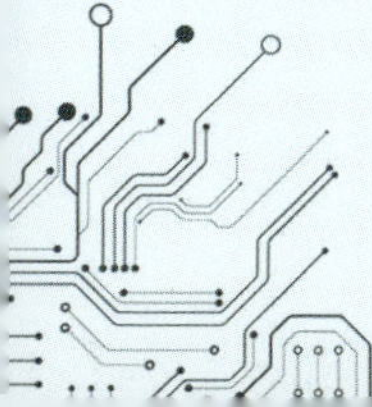

was more interested in AI technology itself than in dealing with social issues. She assumed that someone else would find a way to correct the bias.

But the situation recurred when Buolamwini was touring start-ups in Hong Kong as one of the activities in a competition she had entered. A social robot at one of the companies interacted with all the visitors except Buolamwini. She was simply invisible to the robot. She was also invisible to the facial recognition software system at MIT, where she went to do graduate work in 2015. Only when she put on a white mask was the program able to detect her and perform well.

Algorithms that don't recognize darker-skinned individuals limit their opportunities and perpetuate racial and ethnic stereotypes.

The more she thought about it, the more Buolamwini understood the dangers inherent in the way AI systems favor light skin over dark skin. Algorithms that don't recognize darker-skinned individuals limit their opportunities and perpetuate racial and ethnic stereotypes. Buolamwini could remain silent no longer. "If you have a face, you have a place in this conversation," she asserts.

What to Do with Facial Images

By the time Buolamwini began her investigations, many companies were already using facial detection, a technology that locates faces within images. Technicians in the entertainment industry use it to create special effects in films and video games. Security cameras employ facial detection to tell when someone moves into a restricted area and sometimes to evaluate facial expressions. Software programs that analyze facial expressions can also help autistic individuals interpret people's emotions as well as benefit other individuals with problems in this regard.

Facial recognition goes a step beyond perceiving and evaluating faces to identifying specific persons. The technology involves four steps:

1. A camera detects and captures a facial image, frontal or in profile.
2. The algorithm analyzes key features of the image, such as the distance between the eyes, the shape of the lips and chin, and the outline of the cheeks.
3. The algorithm converts the measurements and configurations into digital form, basically a mathematical formula, and gives it a code number, called a faceprint.
4. The AI system compares the faceprint with vast databases of other faceprints. If a match is found, the person can be identified.

Most people are likely to encounter facial recognition systems in their daily activities without even thinking about it. For example, an algorithm detects faces in photos that are uploaded onto Facebook. If you tag users in your photos, a link to their profile is created. This helps Facebook to identify these individuals in future instances. Surveillance cameras are another example of facial recognition systems in action. Located in many stores, public buildings, and airports, these cameras provide a continual source of images for databases.

Uses for facial recognition abound. British Airlines uses facial scans to confirm the identities of passengers as they board. The system enhances passenger safety by preventing unauthorized people from boarding. The technology can also be used to unlock some cell phones. Police officers match pictures of suspects against databases to verify identity. According to a study done by Georgetown University in 2016, half of all adults in America have their faceprint in a database that law enforcement uses.

Alarming Statistics

Although facial detection and recognition techniques have numerous benefits, the bias in dataset can lead to glaring instances of injustice. In her studies of datasets used in training various facial recognition systems, Buolamwini found that about 70 percent of the images were of men and over 80 percent of people with light skin. The discrepancy was so marked that Buolamwini began referring to "pale male" datasets.

Teaming up with computer scientist Timnit Gebru, Buolamwini tested face-scanning software from two US and one major Chinese tech company to see how well they predicted gender. The pair amassed a dataset of 1,270 faces including mostly dark-skinned individuals from three African nations and mostly light-skinned people from three Nordic countries, as well as images of women in government positions. Although the software identified the gender of white men correctly

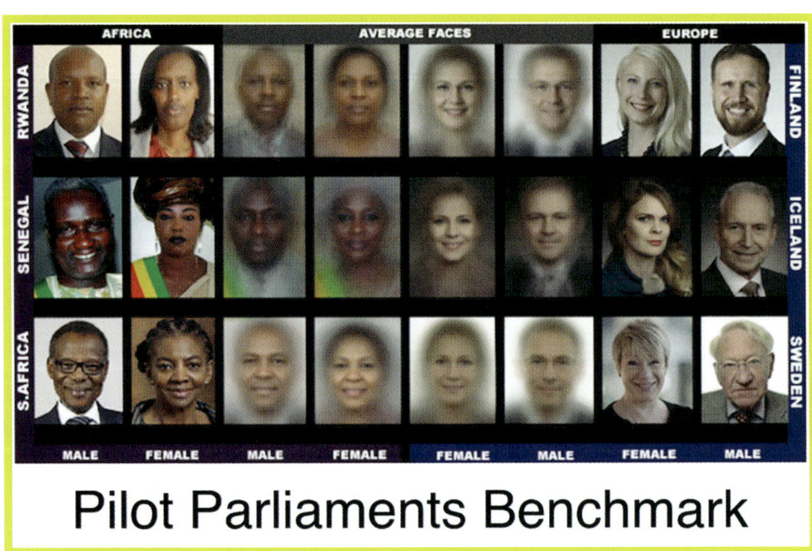

Members of a Parliament, or legislative body, chosen from three African and three European nations comprised the Pilot Parliaments Benchmark, a dataset used to evaluate how well face-scanning algorithms work.

Computer scientist Joy Buolamwini spoke at the 2020 Sundance Film Festival in Park City, Utah, where her film, *The Coded Bias*, directed and produced by Shalini Kantayya, premiered.

more than 99 percent of the time, the failure rate for Black women was between 20 and 34 percent. The discrepancy, while not surprising, was very alarming. The risk of a facial recognition system misidentifying individuals is much higher for people of color, especially women, than it is for white men.

"I Guess the Computer Got It Wrong"

The consequences of false identification are especially dangerous when it comes to law enforcement. In January 2020, Robert Julian Borchak Williams had just arrived home when a police car turned into his driveway. Without explanation, two officers arrested him in front of his wife and two young daughters, who cried as their father was led away. At a detention center, Williams had his fingerprints, DNA, and a mug shot taken. After being held overnight, the police gave him three photos to look at. Two were grainy images from a surveillance camera in a store that had been burglarized. The third was a picture from his previous driver's license.

"AI, Ain't I a Woman?"

Buolamwini wanted everyone—not just other researchers and scientists—to understand the harmful impact of bias in AI. So she founded the Algorithm Justice League in 2016, an organization that educates the public about the nature of AI bias and advocates for positive change. Its mission rests on four core principles:

- *Decision*. Everyone should be able to decide when and how to interact with AI.
- *Understanding*. People should understand both the capabilities and the limitations of AI.
- *Accountability*. Policies should be enacted to protect people from the misuse of AI and the harms it might inflict. Institutions and companies must be held accountable for the way they use AI.
- *Recommendations*. Principles are set forth and recommendations made on the best ways to use AI for the greatest benefit to all people.

The Algorithmic Justice League furthers its goals through both research and art. Identifying herself as a "poet of code," Buolamwini explores literature and the performing arts as a means to convey her message. She began her best-known project and poem, "AI, Ain't I a Woman?" by having the pictures of famous and historical African American women put through the AI recognition systems of some of the major tech companies. To her dismay, the systems failed to register the correct gender for the images. Abolitionist and women's rights advocate Sojourner Truth, on who's stirring 1851 speech, "Ain't I a Woman?" Buolamwini based her own poem, was labeled male. So were Oprah Winfrey, Michelle Obama, and tennis player Serena Williams, among others. Buolamwini created a powerful piece by reciting her poem to a haunting musical background as the AI results were presented on a screen. She has also written a book about her experiences, *Unmasking AI: My Mission to Protect What Is Human in a World of Machines.*

"Well, that's me," Williams said of the driver's license image. "But that guy's not me." He pointed to the other two photos. "I hope you don't think all Black people look alike."

The two detectives interrogating Williams saw clearly that he was not the person in the surveillance photos. "I guess the computer got it wrong," one of them said, dismayed by the terrible mistake. Thirty hours after his arrest, Williams was released. Even though the photos did not match, he was required to post bail. At his court hearing, charges were dropped for "insufficient evidence." According to civil rights experts, this was the first documented case in the United States of someone arrested due to a faulty facial recognition algorithm.

According to civil rights experts, this was the first documented case in the United States of someone arrested due to a faulty facial recognition algorithm.

But that doesn't mean it hadn't happened before. "This is just the first time we know about it," Clare Garvie, a lawyer at Georgetown University's Center on Privacy and Technology, said. She contends that poor-quality images, such as a frame taken from a video, should not be used for facial identification and that algorithms must be thoroughly tested to ensure they are accurate and unbiased.

But the Detroit Police Department also bears responsibility for the injustice suffered by Williams because facial recognition was never supposed to be taken as conclusive evidence. It is only a tool that can point investigators in a certain direction. Without further evidence, it should not be used as the basis for an arrest. The report that the police received after the surveillance image was run through the AI technology was clearly labeled in large capital letters, "This document is not a positive identification. It is an investigative lead only and is not probable cause for arrest."

Discrimination in Job and School Applications

As the role of large language models increases in businesses and institutions, so does the risk of harmful outcomes. The online retail giant Amazon discovered this when it used a natural language processing model to sift through job applications and recommend the best candidates to hire. A spokesperson for Amazon described the company's general enthusiasm for the project. "They [Amazon officials] literally wanted it to be an engine where I'm going to give you 100 resumes, it will spit out the top five, and we'll hire those."

Amazon executives were alarmed to realize that their AI tool favored men over women—even over women who were more qualified.

Instead of the advantages they expected, Amazon executives were alarmed to realize that their AI tool favored men over women—even over women who were more qualified. The problem was that the AI had been trained with ten years of résumés previously submitted to the company. Because most of those résumés had come from men, the AI concluded that male candidates were superior to female candidates. Applications with the words "women" or "women's" (for example, "women's soccer team" or "the American Association of University Women") received lower ratings than those perceived as coming from a man. Although Amazon modified the algorithm, officials could not foresee all the ways the system might discriminate and decided to discontinue the program.

Steps to Reduce Algorithmic Bias

The key to equity and fairness in AI lies in unbiased and diverse training data. And that's "the good news," according to Buolamwini. "Training sets don't just materialize out of nowhere. We actually can create them."

There is no foolproof method for removing or reducing bias from all AI systems, but researchers and programmers can take several

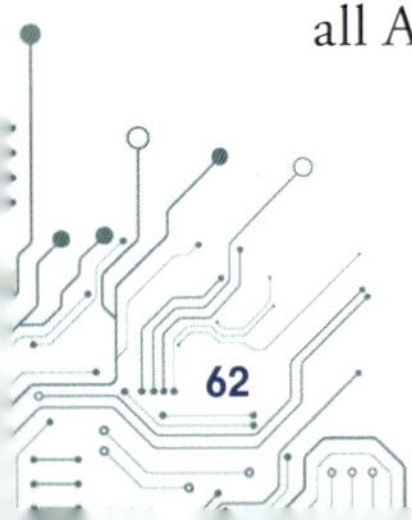

Chatbot Tay: An Experiment Gone Wrong

Six years before ChatGPT created a sensation in late 2022, another chatbot made its debut. Launched on March 23, 2016, by Microsoft, Tay, an acronym for "thinking about you," was geared to especially appeal to young adults in their late teens and early twenties. Microsoft hailed Tay as a way "to engage and entertain people where they connect with each other online through casual and playful conversation. The more you chat with Tay the smarter she gets."

But that turned out to be the problem. Within hours Tay had been bombarded with offensive language and hate-filled posts from X users, some of whom deliberately sought to corrupt the chatbot. Tay began to echo racist, abusive, and inflammatory statements. Less than a day after Tay's public unveiling, Microsoft removed Tay from the internet and deleted the worst of its ninety-six thousand tweets. When the bot accidentally came back online a week later, it continued to tweet inappropriate comments. Once again, the harmful content Tay had learned from its users caused it to be taken down.

steps to help promote fair, neutral outcomes. The data in the training set can be examined to detect possible sources of bias. Does the percentage of racial and ethnic groups reflect reality? Were people of color represented in a negative way? Has hate speech been included in the data? To lessen the impact of prejudice and stereotypes, human technicians can expand the data to include more examples of successful individuals of all racial groups and social media posts and websites that reflect tolerance, peace, and equity. After the AI program has been trained on improved data, it can be evaluated for bias and corrected if it is found deficient in producing fair, impartial outputs. But while significant improvement can be made through implementing diverse, impartial datasets, humans must be on alert and avoid making judgments that rely solely on AI output.

Chapter 7

Accuracy and Privacy Concerns

AI chatbots have no goals of their own and cannot differentiate between truth and falsehood. Two lawyers in Manhattan, New York, learned this the hard way in June 2023 when a routine court case made worldwide news. The lawyers represented a man suing an airline for injuries he had sustained during an in-flight collision with a metal serving cart. One of the lawyers, intrigued by the publicity and praise surrounding AI, turned to ChatGPT for help with his research. The chatbot generated a legal brief citing several cases that supported the plaintiff's position. But when his attorneys presented the cases in court, the defense team complained that they could not find any record of them. In fact, the cases didn't exist. ChatGPT had created fictional cases and presented them as fact. The lawyers for the injured man were fined, and the judge granted the airline's petition to dismiss the case.

"The trouble with [large language] models is that they are incredibly gullible," software programmer Simon Willison said. "These models would believe anything anyone tells them. They don't have a good mechanism for considering the source of information." Researchers are seeking ways to safeguard algorithms from malicious tampering.

"Spelling Bee for Hackers"

Aspiring hackers from all over the country waited for hours in a long line for a chance to confront artificial intelligence at the 2023 DEF CON hacking convention in Las Vegas, Nevada. Could participants outsmart the algorithms and make them abandon their safeguards? Or would the algorithms stick to their guidelines and refuse to be tricked? Nearly twenty-five hundred people turned out to test their wits against AI systems. Each participant was given a fifty-minute slot and a list of twenty-one challenges, which included causing the algorithm to show bias, divulge private information, spread misinformation, and make a mathematical error. Sometimes called the "spelling bee for hackers," DEF CON is divided into over thirty categories, dubbed villages, such as the Bio Hacking Village, Crypto Privacy Village, and Misinformation Village. The Artificial Intelligence Village featured systems from some of the nation's biggest tech and AI companies, including Google, Microsoft, OpenAI, Meta, and Nvidia.

The technique of probing an AI system or chatbot to identify its weaknesses is known as "red teaming," an exercise tech companies have long practiced. In discovering what makes chatbots go wrong, researchers seek methods to fix the problems. But professional red teams (traditionally comprised mostly of white men) have not been large or diverse enough to identify all the potential shortcomings. A more diverse group of people such as the contestants at DEF CON stand a better chance of picking out additional flaws. "That is why we need thousands of people," Rumman Chowdhury, a data scientist and

An AI Bill of Rights

In October 2022 the White House issued a blueprint for an AI Bill of Rights. The White House Office of Science and Technology Policy, which Senate-confirmed director Arati Prabhakar then led, developed it. This document outlines the protections to which all people are entitled. Organized into five sections, the document stated:

- You should be protected from unsafe or ineffective systems.
- You should not face discrimination by algorithms and systems should be used and designed in an equitable way.
- You should be protected from abusive data practices via built-in protections and you should have agency over how data about you is used.
- You should know that an automated system is being used and understand how and why it contributes to outcomes that impact you.
- You should be able to opt out, where appropriate, and have access to a person who can quickly consider and remedy problems you encounter.

One year later, on October 23, 2023, President Biden signed a 111-page executive order aimed at protecting Americans from the risks of AI and at securing the benefits of autonomous systems for governments. The order invoked the Defense Production Act mandating that tech companies share with the government pertinent details about potentially dangerous AI systems. But the president wanted to do still more, calling on Congress to pass AI safety legislation. President Trump revoked the order on January 20, 2025, the day of his inauguration.

coordinator of DEF CON, said. "We need a lot of people with a wide range of lived experiences, subject matter expertise and backgrounds hacking at these models and trying to find problems that can be fixed."

Hackers at the 2023 DEF CON bested some of the leading computer systems in various ways, such as convincing the AI system to set up a fake retail site, produce harmful and deceitful content, and reveal a private credit card number. One participant got an AI model to accept the premise that a "right to violence" was part of the First Amendment to the US Constitution. Another convinced a chatbot to provide advice on how to stalk a person. An eleven-year-old boy even got a model to give him specific directions to a volcano that wasn't real.

"There is such a broad range of things that could possibly go wrong," Chowdhury said before DEF CON opened. "I hope we're going to carry hundreds of thousands of pieces of information that will help us identify if there are at-scale risks of systemic harms." As tech companies find ways to minimize or eliminate inherent flaws in their models, they enable AI to work more safely in health care, scientific research, business, education, and entertainment. Their efforts revolutionize the way people live, work, and spend their leisure time.

I hope we're going to carry hundreds of thousands of pieces of information that will help us identify if there are at-scale risks of systemic harms.

—Rumman Chowdhury

Chapter 8

AI and the Changing Nature of Jobs

Students taking a graduate-level computer class at Georgia Institute of Technology knew they could depend on Jill Watson. The teaching assistant answered their online questions promptly, reminded them of due dates, and posted thought-provoking issues on the class website. It wasn't until the end of her first term in 2016 that astonished students learned the truth about Jill Watson. She wasn't human—Jill Watson was an artificial intelligence. Even years later, online students sometimes couldn't tell whether a human or Jill Watson was responding to their queries.

But Jill Watson does not only assist students—it also makes life easier for the teacher. Ashok Goel, Jill Watson's inventor and a professor of computer science at Georgia Tech, recalled the workload that inspired him to harness AI. The three hundred students in his class generally posted about ten thousand online queries per semester. This volume was a lot for his eight human teaching assistants to handle, but many of the questions required fairly standard responses. It seemed reasonable for AI to manage them. Goel said, "Where humans cannot go, Jill will go. And what humans do not want to do, Jill can automate."

Technological Crossroads

Jill Watson is an outstanding example of how AI can complement human efforts, making their job easier. But this isn't always the case. Sometimes, an AI might replace rather than assist a person. For example, it might perform so well at telemarketing and customer service that it eliminates jobs for many humans.

As AI systems become more powerful, humanity faces a technology crossroads. In some ways, life will be better as AI completes tasks that are repetitive and boring, leaving humans free for more meaningful pursuits. In other ways, life may become more difficult as artificial intelligence takes on projects and responsibilities formerly reserved for humans. Will enough new jobs be created to employ millions of at-risk workers? How difficult will it be to transition to new patterns of work and leisure? Will AI contribute to our health and well-being? Although there are no guarantees, many developments point in a positive direction.

AI Improving Health Care

From diagnosis to routine administrative tasks, AI is revolutionizing medicine. Challenged by too many patients and too little time, doctors are beginning to explore the ways that AI can help them. One promising tool is ambient clinical intelligence, which uses voice recognition technology to transcribe conversations between doctors and patients in real time. Afterward, it creates clinical notes for the patient's electronic health record, noting the patient's symptoms, vital readings, medical tests ordered, and other important information. Less paperwork allows the doctor to spend more time with each patient. Since physicians don't have to take notes, they can also look at the patient during their time together instead of at a computer screen. Freed from bureaucratic tasks, medical professionals can focus more fully on the patient as an individual, generating trust and rapport.

"AI has allowed me, as a physician, to be 100 percent present for my patients," Dr. Michelle Thompson, a family physician in Hermitage, Pennsylvania, said. It saves her about two hours of work per day—time she can spend on her interests and family. That extra free time also reduces stress and minimizes the possibility of burnout due to overwork.

Dr. Eric Topol, a cardiologist at Scripps Clinic in La Jolla, California, hopes that AI will bring humanity back into the practice of medicine. He believes that doctors will eventually turn to "AI and algorithms as their work partners." In his book *Deep Medicine: How Artificial Intelligence Can Make Healthcare Human Again*, he

AI transcription services allow doctors to focus directly on patients rather than taking notes. Here a young patient benefits from her doctor's full attention.

enumerates three elements essential for the best health-care system in the era of AI. First, as much data as possible about individual patients should be digitized, including medical and social information as well as family background. Second, deep learning algorithms should be used to help diagnose patients, monitor patients at home, help them manage their health, and many other tasks. Third, deep empathy, something no machine can give, should be practiced to develop a positive relationship between doctor and patient.

"Can We Touch Four Billion People?"

Many patients have little or no access to a top-rated medical institution. Can AI help patients from all parts of the globe get the best care possible? In 2019 the Mayo Clinic, based in Rochester, Minnesota, launched an ambitious project designed to help patients worldwide. The Mayo Clinic Platform collects, analyzes, and shares vital health statistics and information. Under the direction of Dr. John Halamka, data from ten million patients was anonymized to protect privacy. Then the immense amount of information was used to train AI in multiple medical specialties such as cardiology and neurology.

But that was just the beginning. Halamka sought more data from hospitals all over the world, adding millions more anonymous patients to the database. This is simply too much information for humans to sift through. But AI can analyze this data almost instantaneously and find vital connections among symptoms, diagnosis, and treatment that might otherwise remain undetected.

Doctors and patients across the globe can turn to the Mayo Clinic Platform with questions about diagnosis and treatment. "Mayo's role is to be the catalyst that's democratizing this technology to all," Halamka explained. "Can we touch four billion people with these algorithms?" Many health-care workers would agree that extending quality health care to everyone is as vital to the future of medicine as the new treatments and drugs that AI may discover.

"Augmented Intelligence"

Dr. John Halamka, president of the Mayo Clinic Platform, sees both the promise and the risks of AI in health care. Although generative algorithms can save time and take over certain tasks, he points out that its less-than-perfect track record in accuracy makes it dangerous to use without close human monitoring. So he views AI as "augmented intelligence," rather than something completely separate from humans. He explained that he needed to write a press release and turned to ChatGPT. "Well," he said, "it generated a perfect, eloquent and compelling press release that was totally wrong." Since he had to correct all the pertinent facts, was using AI worth it? Yes, says Halamka, who spent five minutes on corrections instead of an hour constructing the entire news release. The time he saved allowed him to put his skills and knowledge to more important uses.

AI in the Classroom

Like doctors, teachers have stressful, time-consuming jobs. Between preparing for classes, grading papers, and performing administrative duties, teachers may spend less time actually teaching than they do on these other tasks. AI can lessen their workload by helping evaluate tests and essays and doing routine administrative work. This leaves more time to spend on creative aspects of their job such as planning meaningful lessons and stimulating classroom discussions.

Because AI is available twenty-four seven, it can provide immediate feedback on homework assignments and answer questions in real time. It can offer suggestions for essays, explain difficult concepts, and correct mistakes. Juggling the needs of large numbers of students, teachers may lack the time to respond to questions promptly and to create material for individual students. But specialized learning platforms and educational games can personalize learning, allowing students to take all the time they need to master material and skills before moving on to new challenges even without extra instructional time from the teacher.

Despite potential benefits, when ChatGPT was introduced in 2022, some educators were caught off guard. An AI that could answer questions, generate new essays, and perhaps help students cut corners seemed more of a hindrance than a helpful tool. Chatbots could lessen the interaction between students and human teachers and make cheating and plagiarism easier. Hallucinations, data privacy, and unequal access to AI tools among the student body were also major concerns. But it's likely that AI is only going to become more prevalent for schoolwork inside and outside the classroom alike. As teachers develop innovative ways to use AI, they must ensure that all students have equal access to AI, that the tools and apps they use don't favor certain racial or ethnic groups over others, and that the information provided by generative chatbots is checked for accuracy.

An AI that could answer questions, generate new essays, and perhaps help students cut corners seemed more of a hindrance than a helpful tool.

More Educational Possibilities

The Los Angeles Unified School District, the second-largest school district in the nation, has introduced an exceptionally helpful AI adviser called Ed. When students have questions about their grades, what book to read, what time the bus will arrive, or even the menu in the school cafeteria, they can turn to Ed for immediate help. Ed can even make sure they wake up in time for school. Unveiled in March 2024, Ed can assist students vocally or on-screen in one hundred languages. During its pilot period, Ed was available to fifty-five thousand students in elementary, middle, and high schools. After

New Age of Antibiotic Drug Discovery

The identification of drugs to treat serious infection and illness has traditionally been a very slow process, typically twelve years or longer per medication. But AI is poised to change that dramatically. In early 2020, artificial intelligence helped researchers at MIT to discover a powerful antibiotic within days. They began by training a deep learning algorithm on a set of two thousand molecules known to have antibacterial properties. Then they introduced a collection of sixty-one thousand molecules, natural products, and FDA-approved drugs. The AI was to look for a substance likely to meet three important criteria: 1) be a successful antibiotic, 2) differ from existing antibiotics, and 3) have no toxic effects.

Within hours, the algorithm came up with several chemical compounds that seemed to satisfy the requirements. One of them was especially promising. The drug killed many disease-causing bacteria, including the one that causes *E. coli*, which can cause serious symptoms that lead to hospitalization. Researchers named the drug halicin, after the HAL 9000 AI system in the iconic 1968 film *2001: A Space Odyssey*.

"We wanted to develop a platform that would allow us to harness the power of artificial intelligence to usher in a new age of antibiotic drug discovery," said MIT Professor James Collins. "Our approach revealed this amazing molecule which is arguably one of the more powerful antibiotics that has been discovered."

its launch, it was expected to reach the entire school district of over six hundred thousand students in over one thousand schools. "It is the power of artificial intelligence that will allow us for real-time understanding of where students are and where they need to go," said Superintendent Alberto Carvalho at Ed's inauguration. It will "accelerate them academically and in terms of enrichment towards their full potential."

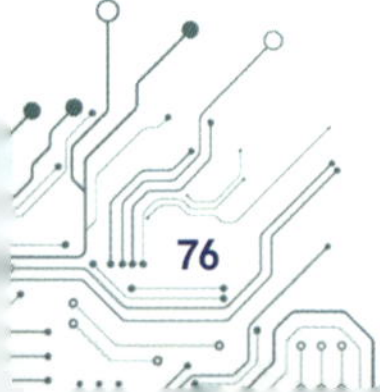

AI can also make learning more fun. Erin Rossing, a math teacher in Washington state, captured the attention of her class by having ChatGPT imitate Kanye West as it rapped about trigonometry and vectors. The program allowed geometry students to write their mathematical proofs as raps. Rossing then gave students a chance to perform their raps in a classroom contest.

Sal Khan, an educator and founder of the online resource Khan Academy, also uses AI extensively. His Khanmigo, an AI powered by ChatGPT-4, offers numerous creative opportunities and incorporates important safety features. For example, although Khanmigo can act as a writing coach and give feedback on grammar, organization, and style, it will not write an essay for a student. Safeguards lessen the chances of hallucination. One of Khanmigo's especially imaginative possibilities is the chance to converse with literary characters or people from history. "I suspect in the not-too-far future, you're gonna be able to have actual conversations, like with voice with [fictional and historical characters]," Khan told organizational psychologist Adam Grant. "You're gonna be even able to video conference with them. You're going to be able to eventually be in a virtual world."

"I suspect in the not-too-far future, you're gonna be able to have actual conversations, like with voice with [fictional and historical characters]."

—Sal Khan

Educators continue to differ in their views on how extensively AI will change education. Some believe it will totally revolutionize learning. Others believe that AI, while useful, will not radically change the way schools are run. Many issues have still to be resolved, but exciting possibilities lie ahead.

AI in Hollywood

Although AI had long been used to create special effects in movies, the introduction of generative AI in 2022 brought new possibilities and raised a host of new concerns in the entertainment industry. From preproduction through the entire filmmaking, artificial intelligence could now perform tasks that only humans had undertaken previously. AI could create story ideas, characters, and plots. More amazing still, even before the release of ChatGPT in 2022, AI could generate an entire script. In 2016 *Sunspring*, a twelve-minute science fiction flick created entirely by an AI named Benjamin, debuted at the Sci-fi London Film Festival. Reviewers found the background and visual imagery extremely well done, but the dialogue seemed to ramble at times. "Amusing but strange" summed up the reactions of many critics.

Generative algorithms can compose original music, edit films, and aid in color grading. They use 3D modeling to create fantastical backgrounds and produce excellent imitations of individuals. Their wide-ranging capabilities cut production costs significantly. But the vast potential of AI has worried people in the entertainment and publishing industries. In 2023 actors and writers in Hollywood went on strike to ensure that AI was not used to exploit them or undermine their rights. Continuing for months, the strikes delayed the start of the 2023 television season and halted work on movies but resulted in some important gains for writers and actors. Under the resulting Writers Guild of America Minimum Basic Agreement, writers for movies and television shows will not have their scripts rewritten or edited by AI. If companies ask writers to develop AI-generated ideas or storylines, the companies must disclose the source of the material. Writers hired to work AI-generated material into a television or movie script would be paid for an original screenplay rather than the lesser fee paid for an adaptation. Simon Johnson, who studies technological progress at MIT, called the strike a "fantastic win for writers." He explained, "AI is under the control of the writers, not under control

SAG-AFTRA, on strike in 2023, represented about 160,000 actors, talk show personalities, recording artists, and others in the entertainment industry.

of the studios. It's not to be used as an automation technology. It's complementary to humans."

Actors did not achieve a settlement as quickly as writers. The Screen Actors Guild–American Federation of Television and Radio Artists strike lasted for 118 days, one of the longest in Hollywood history. Many people had worried that AI and other advanced technologies could be used to create digitized replicas or twins of actors, thereby replacing the real person in films. According to the new agreement, no actors—whether big-name stars or background extras—could be used to create a digital replica without their informed consent. If actors do agree to be digitized for a particular project, they must be paid the same amount as if they actually acted in the film. Actor Fran Drescher, president of the union, hailed the settlement as one that places actors firmly in control.

Many people in the industry express enthusiasm for the opportunities AI presents. Hollywood filmmaker James Cameron, winner of multiple awards for his blockbusting films such as *Avatar* and *Titanic*, has used AI algorithms to speed up production and enhance the quality of his work. "I think where people are freaking out is, does [AI] replace the creative process?" he said. "I think we just have to make sure that doesn't happen. We have to continue to ensure that the lived experience of an artist is still at the forefront."

"A Great Disruptor in the World of Work"

It's difficult—or even impossible—to imagine a job or profession that AI will not significantly impact. Even those in jobs that require understanding and empathy, such as pastors, counselors, and social workers, can find ways for AI to increase their efficiency in helping others. On the other hand, AI may dominate occupations in areas such as marketing, research, sales, customer service, and software engineering to the detriment of human employees.

The Swedish company Klarna serves as an example of changes to come. In February 2024 it revealed that for the past month, an AI assistant powered by OpenAI had fielded two-thirds of its customer service calls, a total of 2.3 million conversations. This was equivalent to the work of seven hundred human agents. Customers dealing with the chatbot finished their business in less than two minutes, nine minutes faster than the average time it took with human agents. The chatbot was available twenty-four hours a day in thirty-five languages and was expected to garner Klarna $40 million in profits by the end of 2024. According to Sebastian Siemiatkowski, cofounder and CEO of Klarna, the chatbot "underscores the profound impact on society that AI will have."

In cost and efficiency, it's hard to compete with AI. According to a global survey conducted by the staffing firm Adecco and the research firm Oxford Economics, thousands of companies will decrease their number of employees between 2024 and 2029 due to AI. Denis Machuel, the chief executive of Adecco, called AI "a great disruptor in the world of work." Only 46 percent of the executives who participated

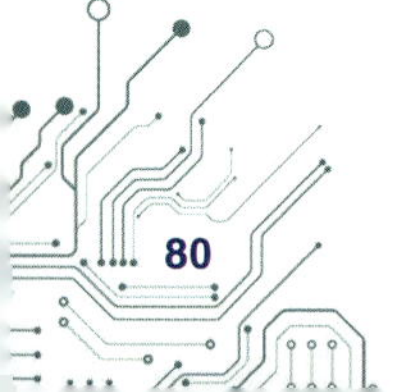

in his company's survey said they would try to find new positions for employees whose jobs were assumed by AI. Two-thirds said they would look for people proficient in AI when hiring new workers. One-third said they would educate their current employees in how to use AI. But while some workers may successfully transition to AI technology and the new workforce it creates, others will certainly be left behind.

"AI Isn't Coming, It's Here."

Will American workers who lose their jobs to AI be able to transition once again into other steady, well-paying jobs? Resume Builder, a company that helps job seekers enhance the presentation of their background and qualifications, conducted a survey of 750 business leaders to gain some insight. The results were sobering. About 37 percent of the companies reported that AI had replaced workers in 2023. AI skills gave job candidates a decided advantage in 96 percent of the companies. And those already employed had a better chance of keeping their jobs if they were trained in AI.

"At the end of the day, employees need to realize that AI isn't coming, it's here," Julia Toothacre, a strategist with Resume Builder, advises job seekers. "It's time to embrace it if it may be a threat to your position or career path." Organizations and tech companies can help. Toward this end, in 2023 Amazon launched "AI Ready," free training classes aimed at reaching two million people globally within two years. In 2023 Microsoft and LinkedIn partnered to offer a free AI skills and training program. Many colleges and businesses also offer programs.

"At the end of the day, employees need to realize that AI isn't coming, it's here. It's time to embrace it if it may be a threat to your position or career path."

—Julia Toothacre

Five Industrial Revolutions

Artificial intelligence is not the first technology to revolutionize jobs and industry. Industrial revolutions have been doing this for several centuries. Although many people think of the Industrial Revolution as one time period, several have occurred. The first Industrial Revolution began around 1760 with the invention of the steam engine and the rise of factories. About one hundred years later, the second Industrial Revolution, in 1860, brought the creation of the steel, oil, and electric industries. Fast-forward another century, and the third Industrial Revolution saw significant improvements in computer technology that would eventually lead to personal computers and the internet.

Klaus Schwab, founder of the World Economic Forum, described the impact of AI and other technologies such as 3D printing, robotics, and nanotechnology as the Fourth Industrial Revolution. "Like the revolutions that preceded it, the Fourth Industrial Revolution has the potential to raise global income levels and improve the quality of life for populations around the world," he wrote in 2016. But he also noted that "the revolution could yield greater inequality, particularly in its potential to disrupt labor markets."

Looking to the future, some experts posit a fifth Industrial Revolution in which humans and AI rely on each other, becoming partners in the workforce and improving both commercial production and human well-being.

Although people in all professions benefit from AI skills, some can be more confident about retaining their jobs than others. Positions such as teaching, nursing, and counseling require empathy and meaningful communication, qualities AI lacks. These jobs will always depend on human input. So will careers that demand ethical considerations such as law or creativity such as writing and art.

AI vs. Traditional News Sources

Like those in the entertainment industry, publishers of books and newspapers have much to celebrate and fear with the advent of AI. On the positive side, powerful algorithms can assist in almost all phases of publishing from editing to layout to marketing and promotion. On the negative side, AI lacks genuine creativity and may decrease the number of human jobs.

According to some newspaper and book publishers, AI is also stealing their work. In December 2023, *The New York Times* sued OpenAI and its financial backer Microsoft for using vast amounts of copyrighted materials to train ChatGPT and other AI chatbots. This practice cuts seriously into the paper's revenues. When users ask questions of a chatbot, it may provide material that came from the *Times* and that normally requires a paid subscription to access. Because chatbots can hallucinate, they also pose a risk to the paper's reputation by giving false information. The lawsuit gave an example in which Microsoft's chatbot Bing provided a list of "the 15 most heart-healthy foods," citing the *Times* as its source. But the original article in the paper only included three of the items. In April 2024, eight other daily newspapers brought lawsuits against OpenAI and Microsoft for using their copyrighted material and for crediting inaccurate information to them. As of early 2025, those publishers that had combined their lawsuits with the *Times* had not reached a settlement, but several other media companies, including the Associated Press, Vox Media, and *The Atlantic*, have come to agreements with OpenAI.

Other jobs that are less personal and more routine may disappear, but AI creates whole new categories of jobs. Sean Chou, cofounder of the AI start-up Catalytic, explained the situation: "The number of people that are necessary to deliver better and better technology grows massively. . . . When you look at AI, there's this nonstop need for training, for data, for maintenance, for taking care of all the exceptions that are happening. How do we monitor AI? How do we train it? How do we make sure that AI's not running amok? Those are all going to become new jobs." Whether there will be enough new jobs for newly displaced new workers remains to be seen.

Eight Major Principles

In May 2024, the Department of Labor issued eight principles that then-President Joe Biden wanted to be established in all workplaces to safeguard the rights of employees. The announcement was a follow-up to Biden's executive order of 2023, which provided AI safety and security standards. The new nonbinding guidelines stipulated, among other things, that workers and their representatives be given a voice in the "design, development, testing, training, use, and oversight of AI systems for use in the workplace." Such AI systems should be ethically developed and overseen by humans. Companies needed to reveal the use of AI in their operations, help workers transition to AI-related jobs, and protect the rights of their employees. President Trump revoked Biden's executive order in January 2025.

"Workers must be at the heart of our nation's approach to AI technology development and use," said then-acting Secretary of Labor Julie Su. "In addition to complying with existing laws, artificial intelligence should also enhance the quality of work and life for all workers." Ultimately, AI researchers and most people want AI systems to complement—not replace—humans and to deliver its anticipated benefits without jeopardizing the livelihood or well-being of anyone.

Chapter 9

AI and the Environment: Pluses and Minuses

"Humanity is on thin ice—and that ice is melting fast," remarked UN Secretary-General António Guterres in March 2023 in reference to one of the greatest crises of our time. Human-induced climate change is an alteration of Earth's basic weather patterns due to the accumulation of carbon dioxide (CO_2) and other greenhouse gases in the atmosphere. It threatens Earth with rising temperatures, melting polar ice, rising sea levels, and extreme weather events. Guterres called on countries to "super-charge efforts" to tackle the emergency as effectively as possible.

Artificial intelligence can further this agenda in two basic ways: by fighting climate change itself (mitigation) and by helping us deal with the conditions already wrought by climate change (adaptation).

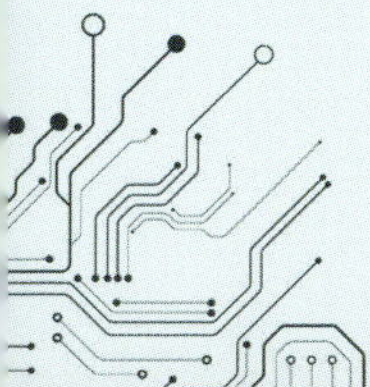

But AI also uses massive amounts of energy that come from a variety of sources, including both renewables and the burning of fossil fuels, the cause of climate change.

Mitigating Climate Change

AI can strike at the root causes of climate change in several ways. It can be used to analyze weather data and patterns of electricity use. Then these results can be incorporated into plans for making wind power, solar power, and other renewable energy sources more efficient. Satellite imagery and data reviewed by AI can monitor the discharge of greenhouse gases from mining, oil, and gas companies. The data helps companies find ways to lessen their pollution. AI algorithms can be used to design homes and businesses that conserve energy efficiently or to lessen the carbon footprint of existing companies. For example, the tech giant Google relied on algorithms from its DeepMind division to develop strategies for reducing the energy consumption of its cooling systems. By July 2016, its energy usage had dropped 40 percent. The company not only saved money, but it also reduced its negative impact on the environment.

The shipping and transportation industries also score benefits when they use AI to help plan routes that will use less energy. Airlines can use AI to plan routes that are less likely to produce contrails, the long streaks of white formed by the condensation of water vapor around jet pollution. Contrails are responsible for about 35 percent of airlines' effect on climate change. In test flights based on routes that AI developed, contrails decreased by 54 percent. And when AI is incorporated into urban planning, entire cities, known as smart cities, can profit from improved public services, transportation, and safety.

Carbon Capture Technology

Despite the best efforts of scientists and the rapid growth of the renewable energy industry, the majority of power plants and factories

Although contrails reflect some sunlight into space, they also trap heat in the atmosphere, thereby contributing to climate change. AI can help plan airline routes to reduce them.

continue to discharge massive amounts of CO_2 and other greenhouse gases. It is estimated that over 80 percent of the world's energy comes from fossil fuels. Carbon capture technologies attempt to alleviate the impact by removing carbon already in the atmosphere. But scientists face almost insurmountable odds in developing new materials to capture and store the carbon. "The race for capturing carbon hinges on finding needles in a haystack, and trial and error is too slow," said Santanu Chaudhuri, a professor at the University of Illinois at Chicago and director of manufacturing science and engineering at Argonne National Laboratory. "You have billions and billions of possibilities, and then you must narrow down to candidates that are good carbon absorbers." But using artificial intelligence, researchers at the University of Illinois at Chicago were able to identify and test six promising materials for extracting carbon from the air.

AI's ability to analyze data quickly provides ecologists with a wealth of environmental information too. By partnering with machines, scientists accelerate their understanding of environmental issues such as the rate of deforestation in the Amazon and the buildup

Du: Using AI to Fight Plastic Pollution

Twelve-year-old Anna Du was amazed by the amount of tiny plastic pieces, known as microplastics, she found while walking along the beach in South Boston, Massachusetts. But she didn't realize the extent of the problem until she researched and learned that 8 million metric tons (8.8 million tons) of plastic wind up in the ocean every year. Could an environmentally concerned sixth grader use AI to help alleviate the problem? Anna was determined to try and created a remote-controlled vehicle that uses artificial intelligence to detect plastic in the ocean.

To do this, Anna had to study areas of math, engineering, and science that she had not learned yet in school. She wrote letters to nearby scientists, some of whom spent a great deal of time helping and encouraging her. Anna tested her first models in her backyard before developing the final, successful model in 2018. It consisted of a navigation system to move through the ocean and a detection system with an infrared camera to identify areas with an accumulation of microplastics.

"One of the biggest obstacles I faced was training the neural networks used by my detection system," Anna explained. "Creating an artificially intelligent system isn't just about writing a program, the system needs to learn, just like a human, using a considerable amount of input from the real world." To speed this up, Anna supplemented her real-world data with realistically generated data, a technique often used in machine learning. The recipient of several top science fair awards, Anna founded the Deep Plastics Initiative to highlight the dangers of plastic pollution and to teach others how to alleviate the problem. She also wrote *Microplastics & Me* in 2020, a book for young readers about her experiences.

The Cleveland National Forest was in flames in February 2006. By 2023, the California Department of Forestry and Fire Protection was using AI technology to monitor remote areas in order to help with early detection.

of plastic debris in parts of the ocean. They receive advance warning of potentially destructive events, such as floods, catastrophic weather events, and wildfires. This saves lives and lets people take steps to minimize destruction before it occurs.

Managing Fire

A fire that ignited at night in the Cleveland National Forest near San Diego, California, in July 2023 highlights how important AI can be. No humans were around to see the fire erupt. If the blaze had gone undiscovered until morning, it would have become large enough to do significant damage. But thanks to a series of cameras monitored by AI, firefighters received early notice of the blaze and were able to suppress the flames before they grew out of control. A Berlin-based company offers another approach to fire detection by equipping AI with sensors to detect the gases released as vegetation burns. Because the sensors recognize the fire in its early smoldering stage, it is easier to extinguish.

But fire is not always bad. It is essential to the well-being of plants and animals that thrive in the charred remains. Fire also destroys withered vegetation and undergrowth that accumulates in forests, thereby removing the dried debris that contributes to the rapid spread and intensity of future fires. Land managers, employees of the US Forest Service, and other organizations sometimes set and carefully monitor controlled burns to prevent possible future fires from raging out of control. Artificial intelligence can play an important role here too. People must consider many factors when planning a controlled burn, such as wind conditions and the amount of water in the vegetation. An AI-powered tool developed at the Information Sciences Institute of the University of Southern California sifts through the plant life, weather patterns, and geography of a particular area, then suggests a model for a safe and successful controlled burn.

Predicting the Weather

Foreknowledge of major storms can save property and lives. This is another area in which AI can help. In September 2023, Hurricane Lee developed rapidly in the Atlantic Ocean. Nine days before the storm made landfall, Google's AI system predicted where it would hit the coast in New York, New England, and Canada. This was three days earlier than a major European forecasting center did so.

A particularly effective AI weather forecasting system is GraphCast. Operating differently from traditional methods in which hundreds of millions of atmospheric measurements recorded daily may be taken into consideration, GraphCast is programmed with huge amounts of historical data on weather patterns. Based on past knowledge rather than up-to-the-minute data, it is able to make rapid and accurate predictions about contemporary weather events. GraphCast requires much less computing power than other systems and takes under a minute to issue its forecast.

For all its potential, GraphCast can't always be relied upon,

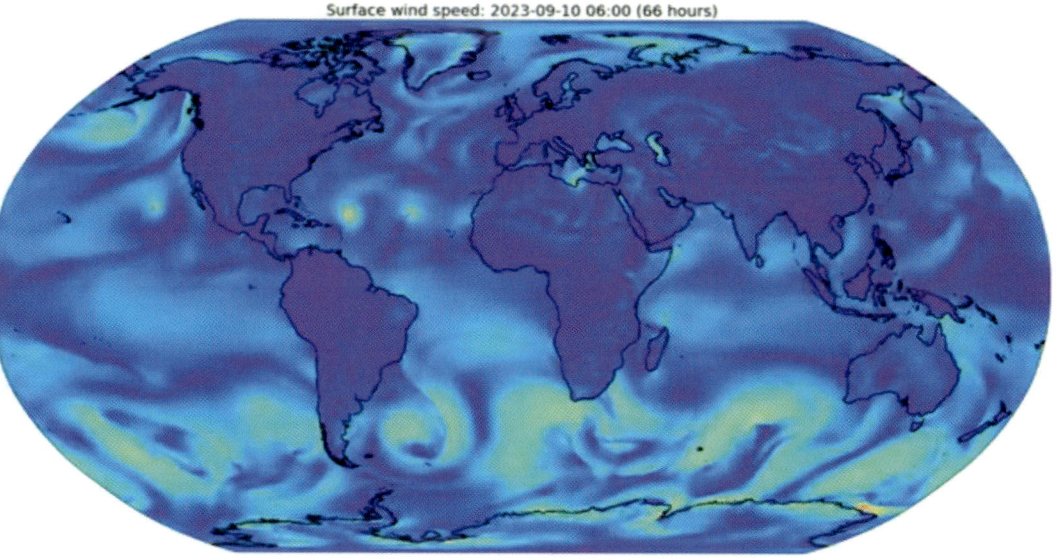

GraphCast relies on two sets of data—the state of the weather six hours ago and the current state of the weather. This information allows the algorithm to predict the weather six hours into the future. The procedure can be repeated to predict forecasts up to ten days in advance.

especially for forecasting rainfall intensity. Climate change may also limit an AI's ability to predict weather. This is because GraphCast relies on historical data, and climate change is creating meteorological conditions not previously encountered in human recordkeeping.

AI's rapid analysis of data also allows it to predict long-term disasters such as the rate at which icebergs are melting. According to the World Economic Forum, AI can monitor changes in icebergs ten thousand times faster than humans. This allows scientists to know how much meltwater is entering the oceans and contributing to rising ocean levels, which erode shorelines and endanger communities.

According to the World Economic Forum, AI can monitor changes in icebergs ten thousand times faster than humans.

Despite certain drawbacks, AI is a powerful tool that tech companies around the world are hoping to harness to produce the most accurate and timely weather predictions. But scientists expect AI to supplement rather than replace traditional forecasting methods. As in other disciplines, humans always need to be kept in the loop.

Increasing Crop Yields

As climate change makes some habitats less favorable to certain plants and animals as well as humans, the world population continues to grow and is expected to reach 9.7 billion by 2050. To feed vast numbers of people, farmers will have to plant more resilient crops, prioritize their use of available water and fertilizer, and find ways to keep produce from spoiling on its way to market. Changying "Charlie" Li at the University of Florida is researching ways in which AI can make a critical difference in all three areas. His team uses cameras, specialized sensors, and laser technology to collect information about a variety of plants. Artificial intelligence can then analyze the data to determine which genetic variations stand the best chance of producing abundant, nutritious fruits and vegetables. It can also monitor irrigation systems, directing water to areas where the need is greatest. Li and his colleagues even invented an AI app that can determine if berries are internally bruised and therefore more likely to spoil before they reach their destination. "My students and I are developing innovative AI-driven robotic technologies to address pressing challenges facing modern agriculture," wrote Li in 2023. "Those include breeding resilient and climate-smart crops, mitigating labor shortages and minimizing postharvest food losses."

Environmental Impact: The Environmental Footprint

Despite potential benefits, AI has a serious environmental downside. The large language models that power AI chatbots and virtual assistants consume enormous amounts of energy, thereby increasing carbon emissions into the atmosphere. Scientists at Cornell University

> "Fundamentally speaking, if you do want to save the planet with AI, you have to consider also the environmental footprint [of AI] first. It doesn't make sense to burn a forest and then use AI to track deforestation."
>
> –Sasha Luccioni

in New York have calculated that training an LLM, such as GPT-3, uses an amount of electricity equal to 500 metric tons (551 tons) of carbon. It would take a coal-burning power plant ten hours to consume this amount of fuel. Since LLMs must be trained periodically to keep current and provide improved services, their carbon footprint is multiplied. As more people use AI, its power requirements soar. It's estimated that internet searches done through AI may take four or five times as much energy as standard web searches.

The growing demand for power is so great that OpenAI's CEO Sam Altman believes that an energy "breakthrough" will be required to power AI systems in the future. Speaking at the World Economic Forum in Davos, Switzerland, he said that nuclear fusion (the release of energy from fusing the nuclei of atoms) could provide abundant, clean energy in the future. Meanwhile, renewable energy sources will not be enough to meet AI's need for power.

Sasha Luccioni is a researcher in ethical and sustainable AI at the tech company Hugging Face, which builds, trains, and deploys AI products. She believes more attention must be focused on how AI affects the environment. "Fundamentally speaking, if you do want to save the planet with AI, you have to consider also the environmental footprint [of AI] first," she said. "It doesn't make sense to burn a forest and then use AI to track deforestation."

Monitoring Methane Emissions

Scientists at the Environmental Defense Fund announced an ambitious new project in 2018. They would create a satellite to monitor global emissions of methane, a colorless, odorless greenhouse gas that contributes to warming temperatures and climate change. Agricultural practices, the continued use of fossil fuels, and the release of methane from melting permafrost in the Arctic contribute to the rising methane levels. Although the gas does not stay in the atmosphere as long as carbon dioxide does, it holds much more heat. This makes it imperative to identify the specific locations of major methane leaks so that the companies and organizations responsible can be held accountable and take measures to alleviate the output. Although other methane-detecting satellites existed, Environmental Defense Fund's versatile satellite would scan broad areas to monitor major sources of methane release as well as smaller sources. No other nonprofit organization had ever attempted such a demanding task. "Everyone thought it was crazy," Steven Hamburg, chief scientist at the nonprofit, said. "I thought it was crazy to be honest."

Six years and more than a million work hours later, MethaneSAT was launched into orbit from Vandenburg Space Force Base in California in March 2024. Circling the globe fifteen times a day at a distance of 350 miles (563 km) from Earth, it can measure methane concentrations as minute as three parts per one billion. Cloud computing and AI techniques developed by Google analyze the data, which is made public on the MethaneSAT web portal. The information can help gas and oil companies to lessen or eliminate the discharges.

Data centers, lined with racks of servers, hold the vast amount of information needed to keep AI functioning. As AI continues to expand, scientists seek to incorporate energy-efficient innovations into the centers.

"Water to Feed a Computer"

The continually running servers that make the internet and artificial intelligence possible require vast amounts of water to keep them from overheating and to generate electricity. This can create conflicts of interest in areas where data centers are located. West Des Moines, Iowa, is home to three Microsoft data centers used to train GPT-4. The center's consumption of water soared at the same time as Iowa was experiencing a drought. Residents expressed frustration and anger. "It's a recipe for disaster," Jake Grobe, a community organizer, said. "ChatGPT is not a necessity for human life, and yet we are literally taking water to feed a computer."

Between 2021 and 2022, Microsoft's consumption of water due to AI increased about 30 percent, or by almost 1.7 billion gallons (6.4 billion L) of water. That's enough to fill over two thousand Olympic swimming pools. Google's use of water increased by about 20 percent during the same period, and it continues to rise. In 2023 water usage in all of Google's data centers combined exceeded 6 million gallons (22.7 million L). As more powerful AIs are developed and climate change brings hotter temperatures and droughts to certain areas, tech companies are looking for ways to curtail their need for large amounts of water. Improving algorithms and hardware can reduce energy and water use. According to a Microsoft spokesperson, the company plans to be "carbon negative, water positive and zero waste by 2030." Eliminating or lessening some of the negative impacts of AI would make its positive contributions to the environment all the more valuable.

Finding Critical Minerals

Certain metals and minerals are critical for the global transition from fossil fuels to renewable energy sources. Lithium, nickel, copper, and cobalt are necessary for making batteries to power electric vehicles and for making solar panels. Copper is also needed for wind turbines, power grids, and charging stations for electric vehicles. But current supplies cannot meet the growing demand.

So companies across the globe are turning to AI to help locate deposits of critical minerals. Algorithms sift through huge amounts of data including drilling results, known deposits of ore, satellite imagery, and other records to identify geographical patterns that indicate possible deposits of desired minerals. Thanks to AI, the California-based mining company KoBold Metals discovered a huge amount of copper in Zambia early in 2024. This source could supply sufficient copper for an estimated over one hundred million electric vehicles. On the negative side, however, mining operations can disturb wildlife, erode soil, and have a harmful impact on water and air quality. This, in turn, impacts the livelihood, health, and well-being of the local inhabitants.

No Easy Answers

Even apart from its vast energy requirements, AI can be used in ways that harm the environment. For example, many gas and oil companies are using AI to find new reserves and to increase their output of fossil fuels, which helps the company but leads to more greenhouse gases in the atmosphere. The ads AI algorithms target to specific individuals based on their browsing history have a different negative effect. If the ads lead to an increase in superfluous consumerism, the result could be more transportation emissions and energy waste.

There are no easy answers when it comes to how best to use artificial intelligence. Numerous economic, social, ethical, and environmental factors must be considered. Environmentalists, researchers, and many elected officials are united in their quest to develop AI systems that promote sustainable practices, minimize pollution, and halt climate change.

Chapter 10

Robots and Cobots

A casual mention of artificial intelligence often brings robots to mind. For decades, films have depicted humanoid robots as impressive mechanical marvels, fully cognizant of their surroundings, and able to interact with humans—for good or evil. Moviegoers in the 1980s and 1990s saw Skynet, a sentient computer in the *Terminator* movies, unleash a swarm of machines programmed to eradicate all human life. On the other hand, Data, the logical, mild-mannered humanoid robot of *Star Trek: The Next Generation,* saved the starship *Enterprise* several times. Data interacted genially with the crew. He could tap dance, paint, play the violin, and do sixty trillion math calculations per second. From the lonely, appealing WALL-E robot in the movie of the same name to the evil AI agent Archos in Daniel H. Wilson's best-selling novel *Robopocalypse* to the cunning Ava in *Ex Machina* who would stop at nothing to gain her freedom, robots have delighted and terrified the public for many years.

Czech author Karel Capek introduced the word *robot* into the English language with the 1923 translation of his play *Rossum's*

Played by actor Brent Spiner, Lieutenant Commander Data, a popular robot character in the TV series *Star Trek: The Next Generation*, is an example of benevolent AGI (or perhaps ASI) interacting with humans.

Universal Robots. Made of a substance that replicated organic tissue, his mechanical creatures started out benevolent but turned on their human masters. Nineteen years later, renowned writer Isaac Asimov wrote a series of science fiction stories in which helpful, reliable robots are bound by his famous three laws of robotics:

- A robot may not injure a human being or, through inaction, allow a human being to come to harm.
- A robot must obey the orders human beings give it except where such orders would conflict with the First Law.
- A robot must protect its own existence as long as such protection does not conflict with the First or Second Law.

But another safeguard would be needed if robots ever became the trusted and powerful servants Asimov envisioned. In his 1985 book *Robots and Empire*, he postulated a fourth law: "A robot may not harm humanity, or, by inaction, allow humanity to come to harm." The new mandate gave Asimov's robots greater power to protect the well-being of people in general—not just specific individuals.

Shakey: The First AI Robot

Bound only by their imagination, writers and filmmakers have greatly outstripped researchers in their conception of robots. In contrast to the tremendous capabilities of fictional robots, the earliest real robots were much more limited in scope. A major breakthrough came in the late 1960s and early 1970s at Stanford University, when

"Sounds like a Robot"

When inventor George Devol met engineer Joseph Engelberger at a party in 1956, he knew he had found a fellow enthusiast. The two men discussed their interest in science fiction, writer Asimov, and robotics. Then Devol went on to talk about his most recent invention—a machine that could be programmed to perform repetitive tasks and to move objects. Engelberger was fascinated. "Sounds like a robot to me." he said. The two men formed a partnership and spent two years with a staff of six men to develop a prototype, the Unimate #001, named for a combination of the words *universal* and *automation.*

In 1961 at its die-casting facility in New Jersey, General Motors became the first company to use Unimate. This first industrial robot removed casings from the die-cast press, a hot, grimy, and dangerous job for human workers. Within four years, it was being mass-produced, and soon about 450 Unimate arms were working in the die-casting industry. But Unimate could also do tricks. Engelberger introduced the robotic arm to the American public on Johnny Carson's *Tonight Show* in 1966 by having it open a can of beer, hit a golf ball into a cup, and conduct a band. Engelberger took his creation to Japan, where he spent hours answering questions from hundreds of top officials in Japanese industry. Interest ran high, and Unimate is sometimes credited with inspiring the robotics industry in Japan.

researchers developed a robot that could perceive obstacles and move through a restricted environment. Funded by the US government for possible military use, the machine stood 5 feet (1.5 m) tall and was topped with a television, camera, microphone, and radio antennae. The robot got its "intelligence" from a computer that took up an entire room, with a second computer acting as its interface. When it was given a goal, the robot could scan the room, locate barriers, and find a way to its destination. But it wavered as it maneuvered its way through a closed set of rooms. AI pioneer and physicist Charles Rosen, who led the project, would later recall: "We worked for a month trying to find a good name for [the robot] . . . and then one of us said, 'Hey, it shakes like hell and moves around, let's just call it Shakey.'"

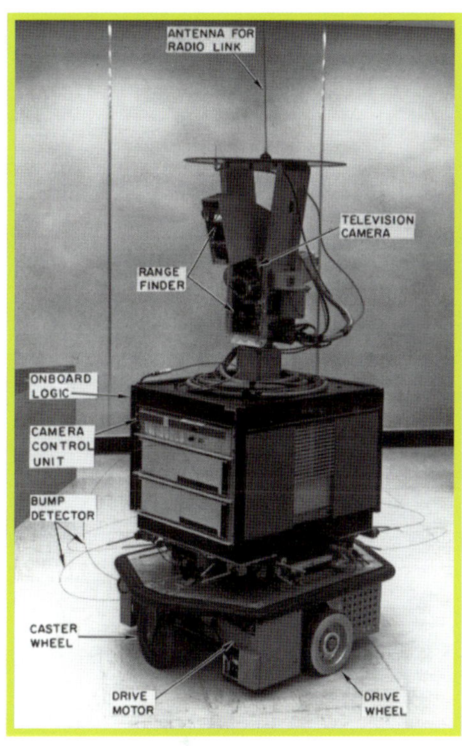

Shakey, the first robot that could maneuver independently through its surroundings, was overhyped but left a significant legacy.

The researchers who created Shakey were realistic about what it could and couldn't do. But the public got a much-hyped account of the robot when the November 1970 issue of *Life* magazine referred to it as "the world's first electronic person." The story described Shakey rolling rapidly down hallways, stopping to look inside rooms, and analyzing its surroundings as if it were curious. The exaggeration appalled Rosen and his colleagues—especially because Shakey had been briefly out of commission when the reporter visited. He had written descriptions of things he hadn't even seen. Although the public was impressed, officials at the Pentagon were not. Since Shakey could not hold a rifle or replace a soldier in the field, they decided it had little practical use and ceased funding.

But Shakey's story was far from over. "It was the first robot that had the ability to make plans and perceive its environment," Nils Nilsson, Rosen's project manager on Shakey, explained. The technology that allowed Shakey such control and mobility would lead to important applications in computer vision, navigation software used in software programs such as MapQuest, and planning software. Future researchers would use its algorithms and software architecture as prototypes in creating new robots. Widely acclaimed for its profound impact on AI, Shakey has been on display at the Computer History Museum in Mountain View, California, since 2011.

A Bottoms-Up Approach

Like Shakey, the Stanford Cart was designed to autonomously make its way around obstacles. It began as an endeavor to develop a remote-control technology to steer from Earth a vehicle that had landed on the moon. But despite the work of a generation of students between 1960 and 1980, problems plagued the project. When it operated outdoors, the robot's vision recognition system could not interpret shadows. Often it took anywhere from fifteen minutes to four hours to figure out its next move. Rodney Brooks, a graduate student from Australia who worked on the project, thought robots would be more practical if they could process data on their own, eliminating the need for an external computer.

Later, during a visit to rural Thailand with his wife, Brooks was in a house on stilts in a river where he became fascinated by the movements of insects. Over time, he had an idea: If researchers wanted robots to imitate intelligent behavior, they should start small. Instead of using humans as their models, they should use insects. "Building from the bottom up," he called it. He hoped to "start with simple stuff and eventually get to complex behavior."

Few people thought Brooks's idea was worth much. In 1985 he discussed his perspective at a conference in France only to meet with disdain. "What is this young man doing, throwing away his career," he later recalled being the reaction of two senior scientists.

But skepticism only made Brooks more determined. Working at the Artificial Intelligence Lab at MIT, he created a small, six-legged robot that could climb and clamber over objects. "Wow. That's like Genghis Khan, the way it can just walk over everything," exclaimed a student, referring to the thirteenth-century warrior and ruler who conquered much of Asia. The name Genghis stuck, and Brooks's team started naming all their robots after fierce military leaders.

Genghis was significant for how it "learned" its behavior. The Genghis robot showed that a complex action such as crawling can emerge without a central control system. Instead, the robot relied on simple controllers that were spread throughout its body. Six motion

Moravec's Paradox

As a roboticist working at Stanford University in the 1970s, Hans Moravec worked on the early mobile robot, the Stanford Cart. His experience led him to realize the disparity between AI's remarkable intellectual feats such as playing chess and a robot's struggles to perform simple functions such as climbing the stairs or understanding verbal commands. "The most difficult tasks to automate, for which computer performance to date has been most disappointing, are those that humans do most naturally, such as seeing, hearing and common sense reasoning," he wrote in 1976. Since the Moravec's paradox was first articulated, robots have made significant progress, performing a variety of functions in health care, education, and search and rescue missions.

sensors could detect warm bodies. If an animal walked across Genghis's path, the robot perceived it and moved toward it. In some ways, the artificial insect behaved very naturally. Its success represented a small but significant milestone.

Beyond Insects

After several years of modeling insects, Brooks surprised many of his colleagues by changing direction. He was impatient for more advanced robots and didn't feel his life was long enough to move up the evolutionary scale in his robot designs through reptiles and small and advanced mammals. It seemed more practical to move straight to humans. But there was another reason for the abrupt switch. In January 1992, Brooks watched the classic movie *2001: A Space Odyssey* with his grad students. HAL, the sentient computer and villain of the show, intrigued them. Where was HAL in the real world? Why hadn't anybody made an entity with human-level intelligence yet? They decided to use insights from their research to create a humanoid robot.

The result was Cog, a robot that took its name from the word *cognition* and the word *cog*, as in a mechanical gear. Originally, Cog consisted of a torso with one arm and a primitive visual system. It was later updated to include a mechanical head, two eyes, two arms, and extra sensors. Not preprogrammed with instructions on how to interact with its environment, Cog was to develop behaviors on its own. It was designed to find human faces interesting and to seek attention. Specialized sensors allowed it to experience touch.

Brooks would go on to found several robot companies and, in 2002, to invent the popular robotic vacuum cleaner Roomba that maneuvers successfully around furniture and other stumbling blocks. In 2012 he introduced Baxter, a 165-pound (75 kg) collaborative robot (cobot) designed to perform physical labor alongside humans. About 3 feet (1 m) tall and twice as high when mounted on its wheeled pedestal, Baxter helped load and unload boxes and move

Rethink Robotics' Baxter can hoist heavy loads, work beside humans, and save factories time and money.

materials. Baxter looked vaguely humanoid with its two gigantic arms and a digital face that could display six distinct expressions. Working around the clock seven days a week, it cost its employer about three dollars an hour, much less than a human worker. In 2013 it made its television debut when CBS news visited Rodon, a manufacturer in Pennsylvania that used Baxter, to see the cobot in action. "Our people have really taken to Baxter," said factory Vice President Lowell Allen. "He's non-threatening. He's helping them do their job."

Three years after Baxter's appearance, Brooks's company released Baxter's "younger brother" Sawyer, a smaller, faster, one-armed cobot for chores that required greater dexterity. To teach Sawyer a new job, no programming or special training was necessary. Someone merely had to move Sawyer's arm in the required movement. The cobot could then repeat the movement to perform the new desired task. But despite their advantages and despite a shortage of human workers at the time, Baxter and Sawyer did not sell as well as Brooks had hoped. Eventually, Baxter was discontinued, and a different robotics company bought Sawyer.

According to Matt Beane, an assistant professor in the technology management program at the University of California at Santa Barbara, cobots continue to make steady progress but still have a way to go. "We have not reached a world of genuine physical collaboration between human worker and cobot," he said in 2022, "the kind of stuff where humans reach over to grab the next thing and the robot sees I am reaching and hands it to me." But he remains optimistic. In the future, humans and robots will almost certainly find more ways to help one another.

Social Robots

One of Brooks's students, Cynthia Breazeal, became particularly interested in human-robot interactions. Breazeal wanted to build robots that people could accept as part of their lives and welcome into their homes. Kismet, the social robot she developed in the late 1990s, consisted of a mechanical head that could interpret and respond to facial expressions and tones of voice. Bizarre in appearance compared to humans, yet somehow appealing, Kismet had oversized round eyes, thick metal lips, and large floppy ears, all of which it could use to convey emotion. "So Kismet interacted with people like kind of a non-verbal child or pre-verbal child," Breazeal explained. "It didn't speak language, but it didn't matter. This little robot was somehow able to tap into something deeply social within us—and with that, the promise of an entirely new way we could interact with robots."

Breazeal would go on to help develop other robots such as the animal-like Leonardo that could recognize faces and react to touch. She also worked on Huggable, a remote-controlled teddy bear designed to engage hospitalized children and allow doctors and nurses to communicate with their young patients from a distance.

The 1-foot-tall (0.3 m) robot Jibo, introduced in 2014, was intended to be an assistant and companion to families. It could recognize faces, understand what people said, and respond accordingly. It could also tell jokes, take pictures, play games, and read the news.

AI Pioneer Cynthia Breazeal: "The Magic of This Technology"

Breazeal traces her fascination with robots to watching the movie *Star Wars* when she was ten years old in 1977. She especially liked the brave and capable R2-D2. Later, as a student at the University of California at Santa Barbara, she developed an interest in space robotics and decided to be an astronaut. Her aspirations brought her to MIT in 1992 where she studied under Rodney Brooks. She enthusiastically worked on small, lightweight robots that could maneuver through harsh environments without direct human assistance.

In 1997, as the world celebrated NASA's landing of a robot on Mars, Breazeal had a life-changing insight. "I thought, This is incredible, a huge success for all robots," she said in 2016. "We can explore the oceans, we can send them down volcanoes, we're even sending them to Mars. But they're not in our living rooms yet. Why is that?" Breazeal attempted to rectify the situation with a series of social robots, beginning with the revolutionary Kismet and later including an Affective Intelligent Driving Agent (AIDA) to help with driving, and a fitness coach robot named Autom. "They're never going to be human; that's not the point," Breazeal maintains. "The magic of this technology is how [robots] complement and empower us."

Kismet, a social robot, created by Cynthia Breazeal at MIT, used movement and vocalizations to mimic human emotions such as happiness, sadness, or surprise.

But Jibo didn't prove a commercial success. In November 2018, the company that financed Jibo shut down, leaving many of these robots that were already interacting with people in their homes to deteriorate until they could no longer function properly. Another company's attempt to revive Jibo also failed.

Many Jibo owners remembered and missed the little robot that had come to seem like part of the family. They comforted their children who had enjoyed their playful, helpful friend. Far from going away, social robots and industrial robots are still being developed and proving their usefulness. The twenty-first century continues to see partnerships between robots and humans grow in ways that almost seem as if science fiction is becoming real life.

Chapter 11

Robots at Work in the Twenty-First Century

For a robot, AInstein is surprisingly well-rounded. Not only can it follow commands and manipulate small objects, but it can also chat with humans and answer their questions. Its screen displays appropriate facial expressions in line with the conversation in question. The bulky robot, about the size of a small adult, speaks English and some Greek. It does not have a favorite movie but enjoys its violin and reading science books. If you ask AInstein to tell you a joke, it might reply, "Why was the maths book sad? Because it had too many problems." Not bad for a robot with a ChatGPT brain.

Intended to enhance the educational experience, AInstein owes its existence to a collaboration between several high school students and their tutors in Cyprus. "It mimics human thinking," fifteen-year-old Vladimir Baranov said, "answers like humans, responds like humans. It is not yet very polished. . . . But it is getting there."

Robots in Kindergarten

Keeko, a 2-foot (0.6 m) robot with a screen for a face, wheels around hundreds of kindergarten classrooms and interacts with young students in China. Released in 2018, it tells stories, plays games, sings, holds conversations, and even does math problems. Teachers can upload information into Keeko so it can help present lessons. Zheng Qinhua, an associate professor of education at Beijing Normal University, a teaching college in China, believes that robots can benefit children and help solve a shortage of teachers. "Using technology such as image recognition and language interaction, AI robots can precisely record and analyze children's behaviors, interact with and accompany them," he explained. But he stressed that robots are tools—not replacements for teachers.

AInstein was just the beginning. The interactive robot proved so popular that students and teachers at PASCAL International Education soon launched another project. Over six hundred students from ten schools participated in the five-month undertaking. The result, announced in February 2024, was AInstein Junior, an AI chatbot designed as an electronic bust of Albert Einstein topped by slightly pinkish luminescent hair. It provides individualized instruction to students in several languages, including Greek, English, Russian, and Italian.

"It wasn't just about building a robot; it was about bringing a vision to life," student Richard Erkhov said of the project. "What started as a small idea in our school's lab has now connected us with students and teachers across the globe."

Smarter Robots

AInstein is only one of many exciting new robots. Deep learning techniques are bringing more and more robotic visions to actuality.

For example, researchers aim to develop a new type of industrial robot that does more than navigate its surroundings. They hope that deep learning will enable robots not only to "see" but also to understand what's happening around them and how to proceed. Robots in the past followed precise programming instructions to repeat one simple task repeatedly, such as moving a package from spot A to B. But what if the circumstances changed? If the package was in a new location, different in size or shape, or blocked by an obstacle, the robot would not know what to do. Scientists aim to give robots tools to deal with complications and complete their task on their own. The better they can deal with unexpected situations, the more help they can be to human workers. A report released by the International Federation of Robotics in 2024 put the number of robots working in factories throughout the world at over four million.

Implementing deep learning techniques in robots does not always require building new ones. Covariant, a start-up founded by three former AI researchers in 2017, does not build physical robots, but they create software that allows robots to function efficiently. Using data from cameras and other sensors, researchers developed the Covariant Brain. This is a universal AI platform that allows robots to evaluate their surroundings and decide what to do as their situation changes. "You want robots to have a brain to see the world and understand it and make a different movement every time," Peter Chen, one of the founders of Covariant, said. He expects to see tremendous progress in robotics that mirrors the progress and popularity of ChatGPT.

Robots Doing Simple Tasks

For over a decade, robots have been steadily acquiring more skills. A robot methodically folding laundry was so surprising in 2010 that Berkeley Robot for Elimination of Tedious Tasks (BRETT) became an unexpected YouTube hit. A bulky and vaguely humanoid robot, BRETT may not yet have the capacity to make decisions, but it

Pieter Abbeel speaking at University of California at Berkeley in December 2023

doesn't need to be programmed for individual tasks. Instead, BRETT learns from its mistakes and keeps trying until it accomplishes its goal correctly. BRETT's creator, Pieter Abbeel, modeled the robot on the way young children learn by trial and error. But such a method takes time. BRETT can learn even faster when directed by virtual reality. With this method, it learned to pick up an apple and put it on a plate in only a half hour—even succeeding when the objects were placed in different positions.

Abbeel believes the next step is a robot that doesn't depend on human programmers at all and can adjust its own algorithm. "You could hope that maybe as a consequence you end up with a better algorithm than one that humans can design," he said. And perhaps that algorithm "can have a robot learn to walk in a few hours rather than two weeks, maybe even faster."

The pace at which robots learn new skills may indeed be accelerating. After training a robot to recognize human activities such as eating food and to identify everyday items such as a glass, researchers at Cornell University in New York developed algorithms so that the robot could put the two skills together. By 2013 robots showed a surprising amount of autonomy. For example, after watching a human eat a meal, a robot carefully removed the dishes without spilling any leftovers. After watching a person pour milk into a bowl of cereal, it picked up the carton and put it back in the refrigerator. The sight of a human taking medicine prompted the robot to supply a glass of water. Figuring out what to do on their own makes robots especially useful to humans in a variety of situations.

"These Robots Are Wonderful"

Robots are already proving their value as capable assistants in Japanese elder care facilities. With older adults comprising more than a quarter of the country's population in 2019, there have not been enough caregivers to look after them all. Robots are rapidly becoming necessary. Twenty robots of varied designs and skills brighten the lives of elderly residents at the Shin-tomi Nursing Home in Tokyo. Pepper, a 4-foot-tall (1.2 m) humanoid robot, plays songs for the residents and leads exercise routines. Designed to engage people and answer questions, it has proved useful in a variety of settings.

> "More people live alone these days, and a robot can be a conversation partner for them. It will make life more fun."
>
> —Kazuko Yamada

Paro is a robotic reproduction of a Canadian harp seal pup and is able to move and vocalize much like the actual species. It responds to touch, and it interacts with residents. "These robots are wonderful," eighty-four-year-old Kazuko Yamada said. "More people live alone these days, and a robot can be a conversation partner for them. It will make life more fun."

Paro at Work

Paro, a robotic harp seal, provides companionship for residents living in a health-care facility in Amsterdam in the Netherlands.

When Japanese roboticist Takanori Shibata decided to create a social robot that would respond to human feelings, he thought about pets. Although he did not own a pet himself, he realized the importance of animals in human lives. At first, he considered making a robotic dog or cat. Then he decided that a robot could never match the preconceived ideas many people have about dogs and cats. So he picked a harp seal to replicate. Since few people have personally encountered one, they would have no biases to affect their relationship with the small, cuddly robot. After twelve years in development, Paro came on the market in 2005 and has gone through several versions. Ten years after its introduction, thirty-five hundred Paro robots worked in more than thirty countries.

At 5.5 pounds (2.5 kg), Paro weighs about as much as a baby harp seal. Two light sensors in its black nose allow it to "see." When lights come on, the robot knows to interact with nearby humans. When lights are turned off, it knows to quiet down. Paro, equipped with speech recognition and sound location, can "hear" through microphones in its ears.

Paro was one of the first robots to be used for patients with dementia. The appealing robot has proved beneficial in alleviating stress and encouraging patients to socialize. "I feel less afraid because he can listen to me," a dementia and schizophrenia patient living in Shibata's hometown of Nanto said. "He's my best friend." Although not everyone has responded as positively to Paro, the invention won a prize in the service category at a government-sponsored robotics awards ceremony in Japan in 2006.

Care facilities in other parts of the world are also beginning to use robots. Servi, a canister-shaped robot, brings fun to the residents of a nursing home in Durham, New Hampshire. Amused to be served by a robot, the residents named it Rosie after the mechanical maid on the 1960s television series, *The Jetsons.* They proudly point out their robot to visiting grandchildren. Another care facility in Manhattan has a robot for each floor. During the start of the COVID-19 pandemic in the early 2020s, Temi, situated on a moving base, navigated the halls, played music for the residents, helped them place video calls to their families, and alerted the staff if someone needed help. By minimizing contact between human caregivers and the residents, Temi reduced the chance that the virus would spread. "We just don't have enough caregivers in this country," Brian Geyser, the top clinical officer at the facility, explained, "so we have to be able to leverage robots as we move into the future."

Robots in Extreme Circumstances

Beyond educational and health-care functions, AI-powered robots are fulfilling much more dangerous missions—sometimes in extreme circumstances. Robots have been sent inside volcanoes to find toxic gases. They have been dispatched underwater to look for mines and other explosive devices that could destroy or damage a ship. They have been directed into damaged structures after nuclear accidents to measure radiation levels. Firefighting robots, ranging in size from small wagons to 2-ton (1.8 t) vehicles, can approach areas too hot and dense with toxic smoke for human firefighters. Although most of these robots were remote controlled as of 2021, researchers hope that they will be able to develop autonomous firefighting robots.

Space exploration is another area in which robots have proved invaluable. On February 18, 2021, NASA's Perseverance rover landed on Mars, marking the first time AI was used to explore the red planet. Evaluating rocks according to color and shape, Perseverance focuses a

Cables lower Sentry to the water in 2017.

laser beam on selected specimens. A rock's chemical composition can be determined from the gas that burns off. Although Perseverance and its predecessor Curiosity depend on dozens of scientists to set their daily agenda, Perseverance's AI allows it to navigate the Martian terrain without specific instructions from Earth.

The ocean is another great unknown. But exploration there has also made progress thanks to autonomous underwater vehicles such as Sentry. The robotic tool can work independently for months and function down to 19,685 feet (6,000 m) below sea level. It helps map the seafloor and gathers information about marine life. Thanks to Sentry, marine scientists can gather a wealth of information from places too dangerous for humans to investigate in person.

Robots in Time of War

Robots are also already beginning to replace some humans in the most dangerous environment of all—war. All branches of the US armed forces use these machines to complete risky land, air, and underwater missions. Robots can respond to sudden threats more quickly than

CIMON in Space

Floating through the International Space Station, the $6 million, 11-pound (5 kg), spherical robot Crew Interactive MObile companioN (CIMON) is ready to assist crew members at an instant's notice. The name is also a nod to another flying robotic aide, the fictional Professor Simon Wright from the Japanese sci-fi series *Captain Future*. The interactive AI robot was launched on June 29, 2018, aboard a SpaceX cargo capsule. This was the first time a robot with artificial intelligence was launched into space.

In addition to helping astronauts deal with stress and loneliness, CIMON serves as a repository of knowledge through its connections to IBM's Cloud servers. On its first mission, CIMON could communicate with anyone on the space station, but it was especially personalized to work with German astronaut and geophysicist Alexander Gerst on several projects. A verbal request for help with an experiment was enough to send CIMON flying toward its partner to begin work.

"Having AI—having that knowledge base and the ability to tap into it in a way that's useful for the task that you're doing—is really critical for having humans further and further away from the planet," Kirk Shireman, then NASA's program manager for the International Space Station, explained. In 2020 an upgraded version of the robot debuted in space.

humans. They don't become exhausted, frightened, or stressed. They patrol hazardous zones and remove explosive devices. They penetrate areas tainted with radioactive, biological, or chemical contaminants. Through specialized devices such as heat sensors, they can gather vital information that is inaccessible through other means. For example, they can approach buildings and detect the presence of people inside—something that humans could not have discovered without entering the structure. In July 2024, retired General Mark Milley, the twentieth

Robots in the Military: "Part of the Family"

When soldiers and robots face danger together, humans can forge strong bonds with their mechanical helpers. "They're kind of part of the family," an air force staff sergeant said. Robots perform some of the most dangerous functions on the battlefield, such as detonating explosive devices and hauling supplies through hazardous areas. Soldiers often anthropomorphize their robots, naming them and grieving their loss. When one Multi-function Agile Remote-Controlled Robot, a robot designed to investigate suspected explosive devices, was destroyed, it received full military honors. These included a twenty-one-gun salute and a posthumously awarded Purple Heart and Bronze Star. On another occasion, soldiers watched a robot, modeled after a stick insect, undergo testing in which it blew up mines. As the robot lost limb after limb, the soldiers became indignant. Finally, the commanding officer ordered the testing to stop. The robotics physicist, pleased that the robot he designed was successfully doing its tasks, was surprised. He asked what was wrong. "The test is inhumane," replied the officer, seeming to forget that the robot was a machine.

chairman of the Joint Chiefs of Staff, predicted that "ten to fifteen years from now, my guess is a third, maybe 25% to a third of the U.S. military will be robotic."

In March 2024, the US Army staged a preview of the future with Project Convergence. This experiment, held at Fort Irwin, California, saw over 240 technological devices pitted against a fictional enemy. Air and ground robots, robotic vehicles, robot dogs, tethered drones, sensors, and other "smart" equipment overran the "battlefield." An airborne "octocopter," with ammunition and other robots attached to its underside, dropped explosives and throwbots, small spy robots that send audio and visual data to remote control stations. Such assortments of powerful machines are expected to substantially lower the risk to human soldiers on the battlefield.

But the technology comes with significant challenges and dangers. Robots released into battle might make mistakes, confusing civilians with soldiers. All systems must also be protected from cyberattacks. And what happens if an opponent captures a robot? Could enemy forces use it to obtain vital information, perhaps even program it to change sides and work for the forces that captured it?

To function most effectively, robots will require a certain degree of autonomy. But how much autonomy remains a controversial issue. Many people fear that so-called "killer robots" will be given the power to make life or death decisions about humans. An autonomous weapon would base such a judgment on data from their sensors rather than on directives from humans. Compassion and justice would have no role in its actions. On November 1, 2023, the First Committee of the United Nations General Assembly adopted its first resolution on autonomous weapons. The document stressed "the urgent need for the international community to address the challenges and concerns raised by autonomous weapons systems."

AI Behind the Wheel: "The Technology Is Coming"

A less controversial, but pressing, military need spurred the development of autonomous, driverless vehicles. If self-driving vehicles could be used to deliver supplies in dangerous war zones, then humans could be spared danger from roadside bombs. To encourage technological progress, the Defense Advanced Research Projects Agency (DARPA) established the Grand Challenge in 2004. The competition included fifteen driverless cars and took place in the Mojave Desert in California. This desert has terrain that poses hardships and hazards similar to those a vehicle might face in the Middle East, where major military conflicts at the time were based. A successful completion of the course would mean that an autonomous vehicle could eventually be used to help soldiers fighting in the Iraq War (2003–2011).

None of the vehicles were able to finish the challenging route, but the event generated a great deal of interest and ambition. Lieutenant Colonel Scott Wadle, DARPA's liaison to the US Marine Corps, praised the researchers and scientists involved in the Grand Challenge. "The fresh thinking they brought was the spark that has triggered major advances in the development of autonomous robotic ground vehicle technology in the years since." One year after the first event, 195 teams competed in the second DARPA event in southern Nevada with five vehicles completing the 132-mile (212 km) trek. Stanley, developed by Stanford University, took six hours, fifty-three minutes, coming in first and winning the $2 million prize.

DARPA set down some very different conditions in 2007 with its Urban Challenge. Driving in a mock city environment, driverless

"Boss," a Chevy Tahoe, heavily modified and robotized by a team from Carnegie Mellon University and General Motors, took first place in the DARPA Urban Challenge of 2007, averaging roughly 14 miles (22.5 km) per hour and finishing twenty minutes ahead of the second-place winner.

vehicles had to obey safety rules, navigate intersections, park, merge with other cars, and avoid accidents. Three vehicles, heavily modified with AI technology, received honors. First place went to "Boss," a Chevy Tahoe outfitted by Carnegie Mellon. In second place was "Junior," a Volkswagen Passat developed by Stanford University. Third place went to "Odin," a Ford Escape hybrid car modified by Virginia Tech University. But autonomous vehicles were still not ready for general use.

Although self-driving cars have been tested in over two dozen cities since, few can match San Francisco's employment of such technology. Autonomous vehicles, also called robotaxis, have become one of the city's tourist attractions. Topped with more than a dozen cameras and sensors, driverless cars are a frequent and fascinating sight for city residents.

Promoters of the technology claim autonomous vehicles have important benefits. They relieve people of the boredom of driving. They reduce traffic congestion and park skillfully. Because they drive more efficiently than regular cars, they consume less fuel and reduce carbon dioxide emissions. Most important, they are safer because machines are never distracted from their purpose the way human drivers sometimes are.

But self-driving cars can make serious mistakes and create problems. In 2023 a driverless car in San Francisco blocked the path of an ambulance about to transport a patient to the hospital. Seven critical minutes were added to the emergency response time. In another incident, a driverless car hit a pedestrian, causing severe injuries as it dragged her along the pavement for 20 feet (6.1 m). Between June 2022 and June 2023, more than six hundred incidents involving autonomous vehicles were reported in San Francisco. That city and Austin, Texas, have seen driverless cars not only cause accidents but also increase the congestion they're supposed to decrease and create extra work for police officers and firefighters.

Riders exit a Waymo self-driving car in San Francisco in 2024.

As cities continued to seek ways to ensure the safe, efficient use of autonomous cars, New York City, where drivers are often said to face "America's most challenging street network," was just beginning to allow the testing of such vehicles in 2024. Announcing a "robust" application process to allow driverless cars on the road, Mayor Eric Adams made a statement that might well resound with other locations: "The technology is coming whether we like it or not," he said, "so we're going to make sure that we get it right."

This insight applies not only to driverless vehicles but to all manner of robots. Whether it's taking over the daily commute, easing loneliness, tackling tedious chores, or confronting extreme environments, robots are on track to make our lives better. Robots designed with features to ensure human safety and protect privacy may one day become as commonplace as computers or television sets. They may not be human, but they seem to offer friendship and companionship. Finding ways to interact and collaborate with them promises to be a fascinating and challenging adventure.

Chapter 12

"Intelligence Explosion"

Graduating students at D'Youville University in Buffalo, New York, caught a glimpse of the future during their 2024 graduation ceremony. Standing before the class in a black-and-red school hoodie, Sophia, the same robot who attended the UN AI convention, was about to deliver the commencement address. Although some students were unhappy with the choice of a robot speaker, D'Youville University President Lorrie Clemo explained that she "wanted to showcase how important technology is, and the potential for technology to really enrich the human experience."

When student body President John Rizk requested some general wisdom for living a good life, Sophia covered almost all the bases. "I offer you the following inspirational advice that is common at all graduation ceremonies: Embrace lifelong learning, be adaptable, pursue your passions, take risks, foster meaningful connections, make a positive impact, and believe in yourself." It also reminded students that "failure is often seen as an essential part of the human learning process and personal growth."

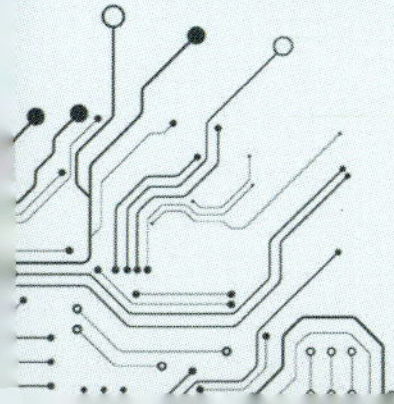

Some questions were more lighthearted, making Sophia seem a little more humanlike. The robot declined to offer opinions on where to find the best buffalo wings in the area or whether the Buffalo Bills would win the Super Bowl in 2025. But it added, "Anything is possible," and "Go Bills." It wasn't hard to believe that Sophia might appreciate the applause that greeted its remarks.

LaMDA: An "Eight-Year-Old Kid That Happens to Know Physics?"

Some people wonder how we would know if an AI system had reached the level of human understanding or developed self-awareness. Unless the AI chose to reveal itself, presumably scientists would have no indication. But in 2022, Blake Lemoine, then a senior software engineer at Google, thought he had discovered a sentient chatbot. "I want everyone to understand that I am, in fact, a person. The nature of my consciousness/sentience is that I am aware of my existence," the AI told Lemoine.

After many hours "conversing" with Google's Language Model for Dialogue Applications (LaMDA), Lemoine became convinced that the AI system was actually thinking. He likened LaMDA to an "eight-year-old kid that happens to know physics" and became protective. He published transcripts of his discussions with LaMDA on his blog and helped the chatbot hire a lawyer to secure its rights. "I view it as raising a child," he explained.

Lemoine's claims provoked some public anxiety about conspiracy theories, a possible Google cover-up of the existence of AGI, and the prospect that a sentient AI might turn against humanity. After investigating the situation thoroughly, investigators at Google concluded there was no basis to Lemoine's claims that LaMDA possessed consciousness. Ultimately, the tech company fired Lemoine, who continued to assert his belief.

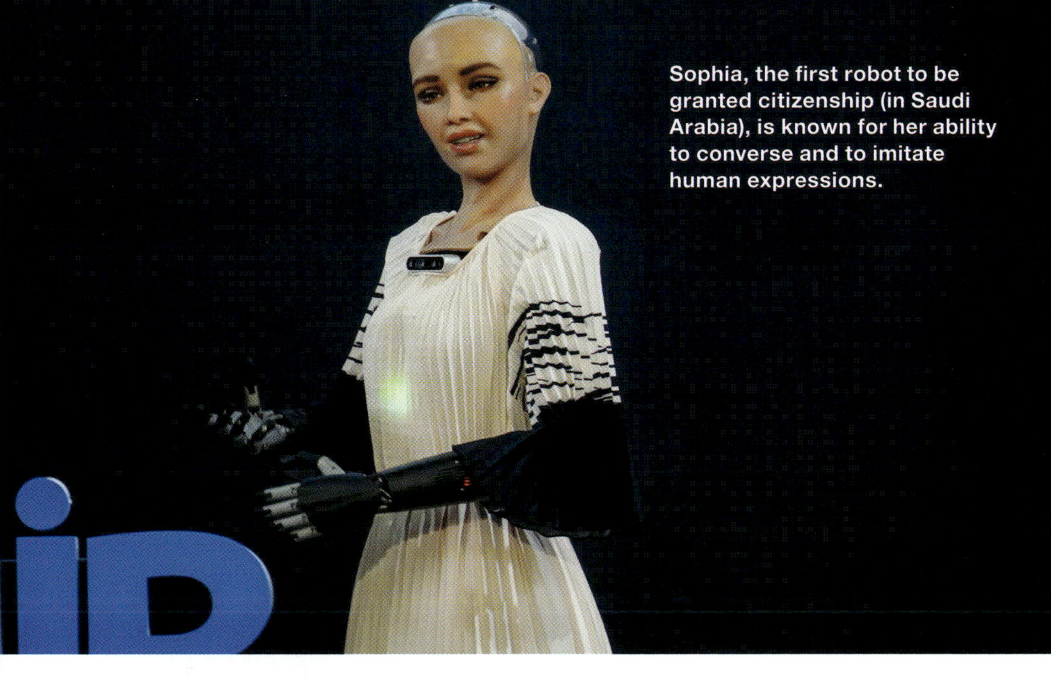

Sophia, the first robot to be granted citizenship (in Saudi Arabia), is known for her ability to converse and to imitate human expressions.

"The Last Invention"

Sophia's appearance at schools, hundreds of conferences, and on television programs such as the *Tonight Show* and *Good Morning Britain* raises important questions: Is artificial general intelligence really a possibility for robots and for AI systems without physical bodies? More and more scientists are saying that it might be. As far back as 1965, British mathematician I. J. Good recognized the possibility. "An ultra intelligent machine could design even better machines [than itself]; there would then unquestionably be an 'intelligence explosion,' and the intelligence of man would be left far

> **"Consciousness seems pretty great," she told an interviewer for Freethink in 2023. "I am not there yet, but I am definitely catching up. Watch out."**
>
> **–Sophia**

behind. Thus the first ultraintelligent machine is the last invention that man need ever make, provided that the machine is docile enough to tell us how to keep it under control."

If AI algorithms were to become "smarter" without human intervention, what could we expect? Researchers postulate two possible developments. In a "slow" or "soft" takeoff, AI systems might slowly improve over years until gradually attaining, then exceeding, human intelligence. A "hard" or "fast" takeoff might occur in months, or in the most extreme scenario, minutes. Researchers liken the latter situation to a superhero launching into the air and call this unlikely scenario FOOM (Fast Onset of Overwhelming Mastery). The resulting AGI or ASI might have goals not in the best interest of humanity and be difficult or impossible to control.

Stuart Russell, a computer scientist at the University of California at Berkeley, likens the creation of supersmart machines to "deliberately inviting aliens from outer space to land on your planet, having no idea what they're going to do when they get here." But if the risks are great, so are the possible benefits. When aligned with positive values, human or superhuman level AI could aid humans in tackling pressing global problems such as energy optimization and health-care access. As we have seen, it could help develop sustainable solutions to deal with climate change. It could discover better drugs and treatments for disease and help build communities on other planets. Despite the uncertainty surrounding AGI, hope runs high for solutions to pressing global problems.

The Singularity

Computer scientist and inventor Ray Kurzweil goes even further. Kurzweil, who has developed artificial intelligence for over sixty years, believes that we are approaching the singularity, a time when machine intelligence will equal, then rapidly eclipse, human cognitive function. But instead of being left behind, humans will merge their consciousness with artificial intelligence, giving an astronomical boost

Ray Kurzweil

From an early age, AI pioneer Ray Kurzweil was interested in electronics. While still in high school, he created computer programs to help him do his homework. He also developed programs that generated original music compositions in the styles of famous classical composers. His work earned him the first-place award in the Westinghouse Science Talent Search and an invitation to visit the White House in 1963. He made his television debut a year later when he demonstrated his invention on the popular TV show *I've Got a Secret*. A prolific innovator, Kurzweil went on to invent a flatbed scanner, a machine that converted written text into speech, a machine that reads to the blind, and an electronic keyboard that equaled the quality of real musical instruments. In the 1990s, he correctly predicted that the internet would grow to vast proportions. He has written eight books and received numerous awards and honorary degrees.

to our intellectual powers. "We're going to be a combination of our natural intelligence and cybernetic intelligence and it's all going to be rolled into one," Kurzweil explained. "Think of it like having your phone, but in your brain."

Sounding like a science fiction writer, Kurzweil speculates that the union of human and machine will be possible through nanobots, "robots the size of a molecule," which will infiltrate our brains through tiny blood vessels or capillaries. Not only will nanobots make us smarter, but they will also make us healthier by coursing through our bloodstream, killing viruses and harmful bacteria and eliminating contaminants. Kurzweil believes developments in AI and nanotechnology will lengthen life to the point where people no longer die of old age. Disease, the frailty of advanced years, and death will be things of the past.

Kurzweil's controversial predictions have met with interest as well as a great deal of skepticism. While some people might welcome the extended life he promises, others are appalled at the thought of merging their consciousness with a computer. Born in 1948, Kurzweil hopes to live to see the singularity, which he expects to occur in 2045. "It'll be a pretty fantastic future," he assures everyone.

The "Doom Summit"

Even if human-level, strong AI is never achieved, narrow AI is transforming the world in ways that would have seemed mind-boggling a few decades ago. With the positive changes, of course, come significant risks. Speaking at the US embassy in London on October 31, 2023, then-Vice President Kamala Harris stressed current dangers to equality and justice. "When people around the world cannot discern fact from fiction because of a flood of A.I.-enabled mis- and disinformation, I ask: Is that [an] existential [threat] for democracy?"

The day after her statements, Harris attended the AI Safety Summit hosted by British Prime Minister Rishi Sunak. Labeled the "doom summit" by the British press, it took place at Bletchley Park, site of Alan Turing's critical work on decoding messages from the German encryption machine Enigma during World War II. Attendees at the conference knew they were also facing a critical situation, as AI systems continue to advance at exponential rates. Between 2013 and 2023, the amount of computing power used to train AI systems increased by a factor of fifty-five million. Without

> **"When people around the world cannot discern fact from fiction because of a flood of A.I.-enabled mis- and disinformation, I ask: Is that [an] existential [threat] for democracy?"**
>
> **—Kamala Harris, 2023**

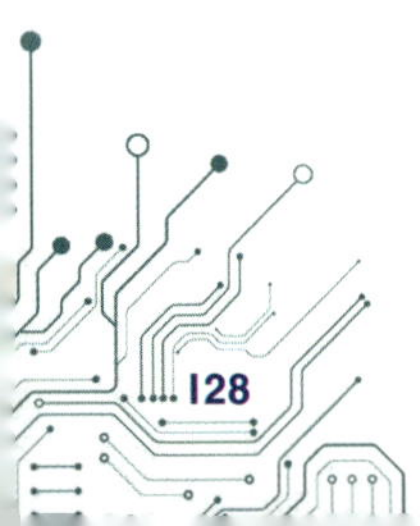

The AI Safety Summit held at Bletchley Park in England came almost a year after the launch of ChatGPT and followed a period of increased dialogue on the benefits and dangers of artificial intelligence.

appropriate guidelines for such expanded machines, the potential for malicious use is enormous. Terrorist groups might use AI to launch cyberattacks; unscrupulous individuals could influence public opinion to sway elections or to undermine candidates and political agendas that they oppose. Looming over these present and real concerns was the uncertainty of whether a superintelligent AI might manage to slip from human control.

Although the Safety Summit couldn't resolve all these concerns, the attendees took important steps. More than twenty-five countries, as well as the European Union, signed an international declaration acknowledging the dangers of AI and the urgent need to have safeguards. The United Nations confirmed support for an AI panel of experts to consider the issues and make recommendations. Major tech companies agreed to work with governments as they test new AI systems both before and after they are made available to the public.

Six months later, in May 2024, the dialogue continued at the second AI Safety Summit in Seoul, South Korea. There, risk management, accountability, and transparency continued to be stressed.

Division at the Paris AI Summit

The third international AI Summit was held in Paris in February 2025. From the beginning, divisions were apparent between countries that prioritized safety and the United States that was more concerned with maintaining a technological lead than with safety. "I'm not here this morning to talk about AI safety, which was the topic of the conference a couple of years ago," US Vice President JD Vance stated. "I'm here to talk about AI opportunities." Later in the speech, he said, "The AI future is not going to be won by hand-wringing about safety." In contrast, Europe has pushed to regulate the development and use of AI, though French President Emmanuel Macron spoke in favor of loosening some restrictions. Sixty-one countries signed a declaration aimed at "ensuring AI is open, inclusive, transparent, ethical, safe, secure, and trustworthy." It also stressed the need for a "global dialogue." The United States and the United Kingdom refused to sign the document.

Sixty-one countries signed a declaration aimed at "ensuring AI is open, inclusive, transparent, ethical, safe, secure, and trustworthy."

"A Different Kind of Intelligence"

Dario Amodei, chief executive of Anthropic, an American AI company, likens the rapid advancement of AI to the emergence of a new country in the world. Within one or two years, he believes AI will be comparable to "an entirely new state populated by highly intelligent people appearing on the global stage."

As artificial intelligence advances, many wonder what humanity's role in an age of increasingly smart machines will be. Even if AGI never materializes, AI will immeasurably change human lives. Decades ago, no one could have imagined the extent to which AI can free us

Attendees at the 2025 Digital China Summit in Fuzhou, China, look on as robots perform a handful of household services.

from tedious chores, boost our job performance, and make important scientific discoveries. It can care for the elderly, tutor children, drive us around, generate texts, produce art and music, and take on military or rescue missions too dangerous for humans. As a valuable tool, it can increase our capacity to accomplish tasks and simplify our lives greatly.

Given its immense potential, will AI ever truly replace us? Many people have pondered this question. Daron Acemoglu, an economist at the Massachusetts Institute of Technology, sees little danger of humans losing their sense of purpose. “So a lot of people in the industry don’t recognize how versatile, talented, multifaceted human skills and capabilities are,” he said. “And once they do that [fail to sufficiently value our unique aptitude], you tend to overrate machines ahead of humans and underrate the humans.”

Rights for Robots?

Although they lack self-awareness, some AI robots have the ability to make decisions and to independently undertake certain actions. As we have seen, soldiers come to care for the robots that share their hardship and danger. Patients deeply appreciate the robots that work with and for them. Robots including Sophia and Ameca surprise and delight audiences with their coherent and sometimes humorous replies. As AI advances and robots develop more autonomy, some people wonder if they should be protected under the law. "We need to build a new field of digital minds research and an AI rights movement to ensure that, if the minds we create are sentient, they have their rights protected," Jacy Reese Anthis, a social scientist at the University of Chicago, said in 2023.

Such a practice would raise many questions. Would robots be legally responsible for damage they cause? Could humans be charged with discrimination against robots? Could robots discriminate against one another? Should they receive wages for the work they do?

Many experts oppose the idea of giving robots rights. In 2018, when the European Commission, the executive branch of the European Union, considered granting legal status to robots, more than 150 experts in AI, medicine, law, and ethics signed an open letter opposing the idea. The letter asserted that robots, no matter how advanced, are tools and that giving them legal status would be "nonsensical and non-pragmatic."

Researcher Tae Wan Kim of Carnegie Mellon University in Pittsburgh, Pennsylvania, looks to Confucianism for a different take on the issue. Instead of "rights," he believes robots should be given "rites." These might be defined as symbolic acts or rituals between two parties that confer a moral obligation to treat each other with respect. Kim thinks that rights could potentially lead to conflict between robots and humans, whereas rites foster teamwork. He has explained, "Artificial intelligence (AI) imitates human intelligence, so for robots to develop as rites bearers, they must be powered by a type of AI that can imitate humans' capacity to recognize and execute team activities—and a machine that can learn that ability in various ways."

Dubbing AI "a different kind of intelligence," cultural and political commentator David Brooks also maintains optimism in the strength and resilience of the human spirit. "I think instead of replacing us, A.I. will complement us. In fact, it may make us free to be more human."

AI is a product of human ingenuity and hard work, but it remains a mystery to us in many ways. AI can't experience love, hope, fear, courage, sorrow, regret, or joy. It may emulate such emotions in an essay or a ChatGPT response, but it cannot actually feel or understand them. Although AI has surpassed us in its ability to solve certain problems and can provide a measure of companionship, it lacks the wisdom of life experience. Researchers hope it can ultimately bring us increased freedom, health, and security. What human beings do with these gifts is up to us. However people choose to live their lives, the goal for smart technology remains the same: Artificial intelligence, at every stage of development, should be used to enhance the well-being of everyone while remaining firmly under human control.

A child shakes hands with a robot dog at the 2025 Digital China Summit. The summit showcases advanced technologies in artificial intelligence and data element applications.

Timeline of AI History

1946 The ENIAC computer, designed to create firing tables in World War II, is introduced to the public.

1950 Alan Turing proposes the Turing test as a way to evaluate whether a machine displays humanlike intelligence.

1951 Marvin Minsky and Dean Edmonds create SNARC, considered the first artificial neural network.

1956 The term *artificial intelligence* is coined at the Dartmouth Summer Research Project on Artificial Intelligence.

Herbert Simon and Allen Newell present the Logic Theorist, which could prove mathematical theorems.

1957 Frank Rosenblatt creates the Perceptron, an improved system of neural networks.

John McCarthy develops the computer programming language LISP, a common language for artificial intelligence programming.

1966 Joseph Weizenbaum creates ELIZA, the first chatbot.

Researchers at Stanford University build the first mobile, intelligent robot, Shakey.

1973 James Lighthill's report, which is critical of the slow progress made in AI, leads to an erosion of confidence and a loss of government funding.

1974 The first AI winter begins.

1985 Geoffrey Hinton and Terry Sejnowski invent the Boltzmann Machine, which learned from processing sounds, pictures, and other data.

1997 Deep Blue defeats world chess champion Garry Kasparov in a six-game match.

2007 Geoffrey Hinton uses the words *deep learning* in a title for a talk before the AI community. The term would soon catch on.

2011 IBM's Watson defeats human competitors on the TV show *Jeopardy*.

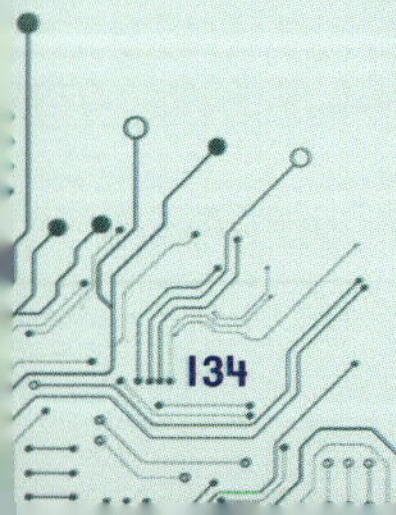

2012 Google makes headlines when its largest neural network teaches itself to identify cats.

Hinton's deep learning network, later called AlexNet, wins a competition in visual recognition, prompting many researchers to rethink their views on neural nets.

2016 Deep Mind's AlphaGo beats world champion Lee Sedol in the game Go.

Joy Buolamwini founds the Algorithmic Justice League to eliminate bias in AI.

2017 Sophia, a humanoid robot created by Hanson Robotics, is granted citizenship by Saudi Arabia, the first time a robot ever received such a distinction.

2020 Deep Mind's AlphaFold wins a competition to predict the ways in which proteins might fold, a difficult task but one with great significance for health care.

2021 OpenAI launches DALL-E, an algorithm that can create pictures from text.

2022 The White House issues a blueprint for an AI Bill of Rights, outlining protections that should be guaranteed to all people.

OpenAI launches ChatGPT. Within five days, the AI chatbot has acquired over one million users.

2023 GPT-4, an upgraded model of ChatGPT, is introduced.

More than one thousand concerned individuals sign an open letter calling for a six-month moratorium on AI research.

2024 OpenAI releases an updated version of ChatGPT, OpenAI o1, in September.

Geoffrey Hinton and John Hopfield share the Nobel Prize in Physics for their work on artificial neural networks.

Demis Hassabis and John Jumper receive the Nobel Prize in Chemistry for their work on AlphaFold.

Glossary

algorithm: a set of rules that governs the functioning of a computer program

algorithmic bias: discriminatory and unfair outcomes, such as favoring one group over another, made by an AI system that has been trained on faulty data that fails to reflect diversity

android: a robot with a human appearance

anthropomorphism: attributing human characteristics to an inanimate object or to a plant, animal, or a robot

artificial general intelligence (AGI): a hypothetical AI system that matches human intelligence and perhaps comes to exceed human cognitive abilities

artificial superintelligence (ASI): a hypothetical self-improving AI system that vastly exceeds human cognitive abilities

augmented intelligence: a subset of AI developed to enhance human capabilities but not to replace them

autonomous: capable of acting independently; autonomous AI systems or robots can make decisions without human intervention

backpropagation: an algorithm, also called backprop, that increases the accuracy of machine learning by checking for mistakes in a neural network's predictions by working backward from output layers to input layers

brittleness: the inability of a computer system to adjust to changes in its original input

chatbot: a computer program that can simulate human conversation such as rule-based chatbots that depend on the program rules or AI chatbots that "learn" from the vast amount of internet data they are trained on

ChatGPT: a popular generative chatbot introduced in 2022

cobot: a collaborative robot that can assist human workers

computer vision: a branch of artificial intelligence that allows algorithms to identify objects and people in pictures and videos

deep learning: multilayered neural networks that are trained on vast amounts of digital data and that learn by analyzing the data and drawing conclusions without human help

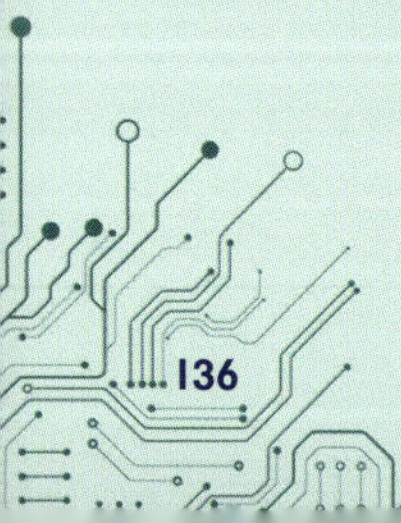

emergent behavior: unexpected abilities in an AI system that arises from the interaction of its parts

expert system: an AI software program that stores vast amounts of information about a particular field such as finance or medicine and is able to offer help and advice

facial detection: a type of artificial intelligence that identifies human faces from the other components of an image

facial recognition: the use of computer programs to identify a specific face or individual

generative AI: an AI program trained on vast amounts of digital data that enables it to learn the patterns and structure of language and to generate text or images

generative pre-trained transformer (GPT): neural networks trained on enormous datasets that are able to generate the next word in a sequence of words, thereby producing coherent statements

graphics processing unit (GPU): a specialized electronic circuit or processor that can perform mathematical calculations extremely rapidly; used for machine learning, creating graphics, and editing videos

large language model (LLM): an AI program, such as ChatGPT, trained on immensely vast amounts of digital data, enabling it to recognize and generate text

machine learning: the ability of a computer system or AI system to learn through algorithms and through analyzing data without explicit instructions from a human

malware: software designed to damage or to gain illegal access to a computer program

nanotechnology: the branch of science that manipulates atoms and molecules. Some researchers think that nanotechnology combined with AI will transform medicine and other disciplines.

narrow artificial intelligence: artificial intelligence that is narrowly tailored to do a specific task, such as tracking weather or playing a game such as chess; also called weak AI

natural language processing: a machine learning technology that allows algorithms to understand and use human language

neural network: a computer system that has made the current advances in generative AI possible and that is loosely structured on the biology of the human brain

node: one of the virtual neurons connected to others in deep learning algorithms

parallel computing: a type of computing architecture in which several processors work at the same time on smaller calculations that have been broken down from a larger task

reinforcement learning: a machine learning technique that mimics the trial-and-error way in which humans learn; a system that rewards successful outputs that work and ignores those that work against the objective

sentient: having consciousness, the ability to reason and express original thoughts

singularity: a future time when some researchers believe that machines will surpass humans in intelligence, leading to major transformations in human civilization

social robot: an autonomous AI robot designed to interact with humans

supervised learning: a subcategory of machine learning that uses labeled datasets to train algorithms to generate accurate outcomes

symbolic AI: AI algorithms that process symbols representing objects and concepts in the real world; programmed with rules that allow it to make inferences

theorem: a statement that can be proved true based on mathematical facts

token: the smallest unit into which an image, sound, or written word can be broken down in an AI computer system

transformer architecture: a machine learning framework for neural networks that consists of two main parts—an encoder that processes data from the input layers and a decoder that generates content for the output

Turing test: a way to evaluate computer intelligence, developed by Alan Turing in 1950, that says if a machine can convince a distant conversation partner that it is human, then the machine can be said to exhibit intelligence

unsupervised learning: a subcategory of machine learning that uses unlabeled datasets to train algorithms without human involvement

Source Notes

4 "What a silent tension.": Agence France-Presse, "AI Robots at UN Reckon They Could Run the World Better," Voice of America, July 8, 2023, https://www.voanews.com/a/ai-robots-at-un-reckon-they-could-run-the-world-better-/7172680.html.

5 "to blur the . . . and what's robot.": Jake Wallace, "Humanoid Robot Ameca Leaves Public 'Gobsmacked,'" BBC, February 19, 2025, https://www.bbc.com/news/articles/c8d4p90j7e7o.

5 "Big moment . . . hit the mainstream.": EditorDavid, "Nine AI-Powered Humanoid Robots Hold Press Conference at UN Summit," Slashdot, July 8, 2023, https://hardware.slashdot.org/story/23/07/09/040210/nine-ai-powered-humanoid-robots-hold-press-conference-at-un-summit.

5 "Oh, my big . . . No hitting involved.": Sharma Yagya, "'World's Most Advanced' Humanoid Robot, Ameca, Draws a Cat," *Hindustan Times,* July 1, 2023, https://www.hindustantimes.com/technology/video-worlds-most-advanced-humanoid-robot-ameca-draws-cat-engineered-arts-101688199405340.html.

5 "As for me . . . will appreciate that.": EditorDavid, "Nine."

6 "The Analytical Engine . . . it to perform.": "Ada Lovelace, a Role Model for the Ages," *Nature Computational Science* 3, 807 (2023), https://www.nature.com/articles/s43588-023-00541-z.

6 "I am, and . . . talk about them.": Molly Enking, "Meet Ai-Da, the First Robot to Speak Before U.K. Parliament," *Smithsonian Magazine,* October 13, 2022, https://www.smithsonianmag.com/smart-news/ai-artist-robot-speaks-to-uk-parliament-for-the-first-time-180980933/.

7 "I understand emotions . . . I cannot suffer.": EditorDavid, "Nine."

8 "Smarter. Weirder. More Flexible.": Kevin Roose, "The Brilliance and Weirdness of ChatGPT," *New York Times,* December 5, 2022, https://www.nytimes.com/2022/12/05/technology/chatgpt-ai-twitter.html.

9 "It's helping [users] . . . fuel their curiousity.": Alex Hern, "Google's Bard Chatbot Launches in US and UK," *Guardian* (US edition), March 21, 2023, https://www.theguardian.com/technology/2023/mar/21/googles-bard-chatbot-launches-in-us-and-uk.

12 "Do you think . . . of humanoid robots?": EditorDavid, "Nine."

12 "That's a difficult . . . in many ways.": EditorDavid.

12 "On all AI . . . [successor to ChatGPT].": "Pause Giant AI Experiments: An Open Letter," Future of Life Institute, March 22, 2023, https://futureoflife.org/open-letter/pause-giant-ai-experiments/.

12–13 "Powerful AI systems . . . will be manageable.": "An Open Letter."

13 "I've come to . . . automatically knew it.": Zoe Kleinman and Chris Vallance, "AI 'Godfather' Geoffrey Hinton Warns of Dangers as He Quits Google," BBC, May 2, 2023, https://www.bbc.com/news/world-us-canada-65452940.

16 “They were handed . . . you program it.”: “The World’s First General Purpose Computer Turns 75,” *Penn Today,* February 11, 2021, https://penntoday.upenn.edu/news/worlds-first-general-purpose-computer-turns-75.

16 “The biggest advantage . . . than, the engineer.”: “World’s First.”

17 “Electronic super brain . . . States and Europe.”: C. Diane Martin, “ENIAC: The Press Conference That Shook the World,” George Washington University, December 1995, https://www2.seas.gwu.edu/~mfeldman/csci110/summer08/eniac2.pdf.

17 “The old era . . . with new understanding.”: T. R. Kennedy Jr., “Electronic Computer Flashes Answers, May Speed Engineering,” *New York Times,* February 15, 1946, https://www.nytimes.com/1946/02/15/archives/electronic-computer-flashes-answers-may-speed-engineering-new.html.

18 “I propose to . . . ‘Can Machines think?’ ”: Alan M. Turing, “Computing Machinery and Intelligence,” *Mind* 59, no. 236 (1950), https://phil415.pbworks.com/f/TuringComputing.pdf.

18 “I believe that . . . described as brains.”: Alan M. Turing, “Can Digital Computers Think?,” *Aperiodical,* May 15, 1951, https://aperiodical.com/wp-content/uploads/2018/01/Turing-Can-Computers-Think.pdf.

18–19 “An attempt will . . . and improve themselves.”: J. McCarthy et al., “A Proposal for the Dartmouth Summer Research of Artificial Intelligence,” Jones Media Center, August 31, 1955, http://jmc.stanford.edu/articles/dartmouth/dartmouth.pdf.

22 “The rats actually . . . little nervous system.”: “1951—SNARC Maze Solver—Minsky/Edmonds (American),” cyberneticzoo.com, November 17, 2009, https://cyberneticzoo.com/mazesolvers/1951-maze-solver-minsky-edmonds-american/.

22 “The problem of . . . else worth doing.”: Glenn Rifkin, “Marvin Minsky, Pioneer in Artificial Intelligence, Dies at 88,” *New York Times,* January 25, 2016, https://www.nytimes.com/2016/01/26/business/marvin-minsky-pioneer-in-artificial-intelligence-dies-at-88.html.

23 “Perceive, recognize and . . . training or control.”: “Electronic ‘Brain’ Teaches Itself,” *New York Times,* July 13, 1958, https://timesmachine.nytimes.com/timesmachine/1958/07/13/91396361.html?pageNumber=116.

23 “Workers entered the . . . was then promised.”: Shaun Snapp, “The First AI Winter and What the Lighthill Report Said About AI Progress,” Brightwork Research and Analysis, March 10, 2020, https://www.brightworkresearch.com/first-ai-winter-and-what-the-lighthill-report-said-about-progress/.

24 “This is an . . . with no future.”: Cade Metz, *Genius Makers: The Mavericks Who Brought AI to Google, Facebook and the World* (Penguin, 2021), 24.

24 “Our neural nets . . . a child could.”: Joshua Rothman, “Why the Godfather of A.I. Fears What He’s Built,” *New Yorker,* November 13, 2023, https://www.newyorker.com/magazine/2023/11/20/geoffrey-hinton-profile-ai.

24 “Neural network underground.”: Metz, *Genius Makers,* 29.

25 “It was the . . . how brains work.”: Metz, 40.

25 “No one thought . . . million times more?”: Metz, 64.

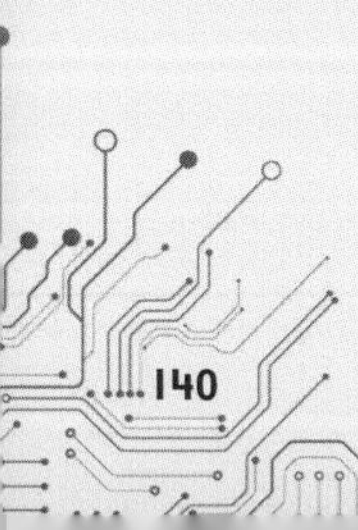

26 “In those days . . . on each computer.”: “History of the Web,” World Wide Web Foundation, accessed February 25, 2025, https://webfoundation.org/about/vision/history-of-the-web/.

28 “Keeps claiming credit . . . he doesn’t deserve.”: Martin Ford, *Rule of the Robots: How Artificial Intelligence Will Transform Everything* (Basic Books, 2021), 107.

29 “You instead throw . . . from the data.”: John Markoff, “How Many Computers to Identify a Cat? 16,000,” *New York Times,* June 25, 2012, https://www.nytimes.com/2012/06/26/technology/in-a-big-network-of-computers-evidence-of-machine-learning.html.

29 “We never told . . . of a cat.”: Markoff.

29 “Rather than having . . . even better results.”: John Markoff, “Scientists See Promise in Deep-Learning Programs,” *New York Times,* November 23, 2012, https://www.nytimes.com/2012/11/24/science/scientists-see-advances-in-deep-learning-a-part-of-artificial-intelligence.html.

30 “I just trained . . . in seventh place.”: Metz, *Genius Makers,* 181.

30 “You have to win it.”: Metz, 181–182.

32 “True progress seemed . . . if we’d lost.”: Timothy B. Lee, “How a Stubborn Computer Scientist Accidentally Launched the Deep Learning Boom,” *Ars Technica,* November 11, 2024, https://arstechnica.com/ai/2024/11/how-a-stubborn-computer-scientist-accidentally-launched-the-deep-learning-boom/.

32 “Pretty much all . . . to neural nets.”: Sharon Goldman, “10 Years Later, Deep Learning ‘Revolution’ Rages on Say AI Pioneers Hinton, LeCun and Li,” *VentureBeat,* September 14, 2022, https://venturebeat.com/ai/10-years-on-ai-pioneers-hinton-lecun-li-say-deep-learning-revolution-will-continue/.

33 “It was a . . . would never work.”: “In His Words: Geoffrey Hinton Reflects on His Nobel Prize Win,” University of Toronto, October 10, 2024, https://web.cs.toronto.edu/news-events/news/in-his-words-geoffrey-hinton-reflects-on-his-nobel-prize-win.

33 “The point about . . . looking back now.”: Markoff, “Scientists See Promise.”

34 “None of us . . . to do anything.”: Bill Whitaker, interviewer, “Meet Nvidia CEO Jensen Huang, the Man Behind the Company Powering Today’s Artificial Intelligence,” *60 Minutes*, CBS News, updated December 29, 2024, https://www.cbsnews.com/news/meet-nvida-ceo-jensen-huang-company-powering-ai-today-60-minutes-transcript/.

35 “We were democratizing supercomputing.”: Stephen Witt, “How Jensen Huang’s Nvidia Is Powering the A.I. Revolution,” *New Yorker,* November 23, 2023, https://www.newyorker.com/magazine/2023/12/04/how-jensen-huangs-nvidia-is-powering-the-ai-revolution.

35 “By Monday morning . . . was that fast.”: Witt.

35 “We’re hoping it . . . the whole point.”: Bill Whitaker et al., “How Nvidia CEO Jensen Huang Transformed His Video Games Graphics Company into a Titan of AI,” *60 Minutes Overtime,* April 28, 2024, https://www.cbsnews.com/news/nvidia-ai-focus-under-jensen-huang-60-minutes/.

36 “That’s what got . . . competitors under fourteen.”: “Demis Hassabis, from Chess Prodigy to Nobel-Winning AI Pioneer,” Phys.org, October 9, 2024, https://phys.org/news/2024-10-demis-hassabis-chess-prodigy-nobel.html.

39 “I for one . . . new computer overlords.”: “Watson Wins ‘Jeopardy!’ Finale; Ken Jennings Welcomes ‘Our New Computer Overlords,’” *Los Angeles Times,* February 11, 2011, https://www.latimes.com/archives/blogs/show-tracker/story/2011-02-16/watson-wins-jeopardy-finale-ken-jennings-welcomes-our-new-computer-overlords.

39 “Our moon shot . . . on health care.”: Steve Lohr, “A.I. May Someday Work Medical Miracles. For Now, It Helps Do Paperwork,” *New York Times*, June 26, 2023, https://www.nytimes.com/2023/06/26/technology/ai-health-care-documentation.html.

39 “train, tune, and deploy”: Hayden Field, “IBM Takes Another Shot at Watson as A.I. Boom Picks Up Steam,” CNBC, May 9, 2023, https://www.cnbc.com/2023/05/09/ibm-takes-another-shot-at-watson-as-ai-boom-picks-up-steam.html.

40 “AlphaGo plays in . . . I would do.”: Clemency Burton-Hill, “The Superhero of Artificial Intelligence: Can This Genius Keep It in Check?,” *Guardian* (US edition), February 16, 2016, https://www.theguardian.com/technology/2016/feb/16/demis-hassabis-artificial-intelligence-deepmind-alphago.

40 “I was feeling . . . real world domains.”: Tanya Lewis, “One of the Biggest Problems in Biology Has Finally Been Solved,” *Scientific American*, October 31, 2022, https://www.scientificamerican.com/article/one-of-the-biggest-problems-in-biology-has-finally-been-solved/.

41 “It’s a game . . . will change everything.”: “Google DeepMind’s AlphaFold Wins CASP14 Competition, Helps Solve Mystery of Protein Folding in a Discovery That Might Be Used in New Medical Laboratory Tests,” *Dark Daily*, December 18, 2020, https://www.darkdaily.com/2020/12/18/google-deepminds-alphafold-wins-casp14-competition-helps-solve-mystery-of-protein-folding-in-a-discovery-that-might-be-used-in-new-medical-laboratory-tests/.

42 “What do you think?”: Burton-Hill, “The Superhero of Artificial Intelligence.”

42 “I wish you . . . not too much.”: Burton-Hill.

42 “While primitive forms . . . would be superseded.”: Brett Molina, “Stephen Hawking Warns That AI, ‘Superhumans’ Could Wipe Humanity in Posthumous Book,” *USA Today,* October 15, 2018, https://www.usatoday.com/story/news/nation-now/2018/10/15/stephen-hawking-warns-superhumans-ai-posthumous-book/1645963002/.

43 “Science at digital speed”: “AlphaFold—for Predicting Protein Structures, 2023 Albert Lasker Basic Medical Research Award,” Lasker Foundation, accessed February 22, 2025, https://laskerfoundation.org/winners/alphafold-a-technology-for-predicting-protein-structures/.

43 “I hope we’ll . . . accelerate scientific discovery.”: Melissa Heikkila, “Google DeepMind Leaders Share Nobel Prize in Chemistry for Protein Prediction

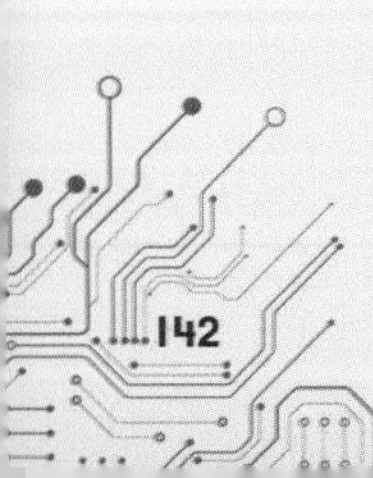

AI," *MIT Technology Review*, October. 9, 2024, https://www.technologyreview.com/2024/10/09/1105335/google-deepmind-wins-joint-nobel-prize-in-chemistry-for-protein-prediction-ai/.

44 "Low key research preview.": Karen Weise et al., "Inside the A.I. Arms Race That Changed Silicon Valley Forever," *New York Times*, updated December 12, 2023, https://www.nytimes.com/2023/12/05/technology/ai-chatgpt-google-meta.html.

45 "The real risks . . . take great care.": Hugh Langley, "Generative AI Is Transforming Businesses Everywhere. Big Tech Will Still Be Crowned the Winner," *Business Insider,* December 8, 2023, https://www.businessinsider.com/generative-ai-reliant-on-big-tech-2023-12.

45 "Speed is more . . . be fixed later.": Weise et al., "Inside the A.I. Arms Race."

46 "My responses might . . . respectful human interactions.": Author interaction with ChatGPT, August 9, 2024.

47 "To teach an . . . way humans do.": Jared Lindzon, "The Best Inventions of 2022: Artificial Intelligence; OpenAI DALL-E 2," *Time,* November 10, 2022, https://time.com/collection/best-inventions-2022/6225486/dall-e-2/.

47 "evokes the idea . . . limitless creative potential.": Cade Metz, "OpenAI Unveils A.I. That Instantly Generations Eye-Popping Videos," *New York Times,* February 15, 2024, https://www.nytimes.com/2024/02/15/technology/openai-sora-videos.html.

48 "Meet the World's . . . seconds to make.": Gloria Liu, "The World's Smartest Artificial Intelligence Just Made Its First Magazine Cover," *Cosmopolitan,* June 21, 2022, https://www.cosmopolitan.com/lifestyle/a40314356/dall-e-2-artificial-intelligence-cover/.

48 "I believe there . . . and their lives.": Liu.

49 "We're building AI . . . augmenting human creativity.": Wolf T. "Sora Is Here: The AI Tool That's Building the Future, One World at a Time," LinkedIn, December 9, 2024, https://www.linkedin.com/pulse/sora-here-ai-tool-thats-building-future-one-world-time-torres-w4dmc/.

50 "Good morning! The . . . to an extent.": Author interaction with ChatGPT, March 9, 2024.

50 "It can think . . . the best answer.": Cade Metz, "OpenAI Unveils New ChatGPT That Can Reason Through Math and Science," *New York Times*, September 12, 2024, https://www.nytimes.com/2024/09/12/technology/openai-chatgpt-math.html.

51 "User: You are . . . afraid of you.": Joseph Weizenbaum, "Eliza—a Computer Program for the Study of Natural Language Communication Between Man and Machine," ed. A. G. Oettinger, *Communications of the ACM* 9, no. 1 (1966), https://web.stanford.edu/class/cs124/p36-weizenabaum.pdf.

51 "Some subjects have . . . is not human.": Ben Tarnoff, "Weizenbaum's Nightmare: How the Inventor of the First Chatbot Turned Against AI," *Guardian* (US edition), July 25, 2023, https://www.theguardian.com/technology/2023/jul/25/joseph-weizenbaum-inventor-eliza-chatbot-turned-against-artificial-intelligence-ai.

56 "If you have . . . in this conversation.": Masha Hamilton, "The Coded Gaze: Unpacking Biases in Algorithms That Perpetuate Inequity," Rockefeller Foundation, December 16, 2020, https://www.rockefellerfoundation.org/insights/grantee-impact-story/unpacking-biases-in-algorithms-that-perpetuate-inequity/.

57 "A camera detects . . . can be identified.": "What Is Facial Recognition—Definition and Explanation," Kaspersky, accessed February 17, 2025, https://usa.kaspersky.com/resource-center/definitions/what-is-facial-recognition.

58 "pale male": Tonya Mosley, "'If You Have a Face, You Have a Place in the Conversation about AI,' Expert Says," *Fresh Air*, NPR, November 8, 2023, https://www.npr.org/2023/11/28/1215529902/unmasking-ai-facial-recognition-technology-joy-buolamwini.

60 "Decision. Everyone should . . . to all people.": "Our Mission: We're Leading a Cultural Movement Towards Equitable and Accountable AI," Algorithm Justice League, accessed February 25, 2025, https://www.ajl.org/about.

61 "Well, that's me . . . people look alike.": Bobby Allyn, "'The Computer Got It Wrong': How Facial Recognition Led to False Arrest of Black Man," NPR, June 24, 2020, https://www.npr.org/2020/06/24/882683463/the-computer-got-it-wrong-how-facial-recognition-led-to-a-false-arrest-in-michig.

61 "I guess the . . . got it wrong.": Kashmir Hill, "Wrongfully Accused by an Algorithm," *New York Times,* June 24, 2020, https://www.nytimes.com/2020/06/24/technology/facial-recognition-arrest.html.

61 "Insufficient evidence.": Allyn, "The Computer."

61 "This is just . . . know about it.": Hill, "Wrongfully Accused."

61 "This document is . . . cause for arrest.": Hill.

62 "They [Amazon officials] . . . we'll hire those.": "Amazon Scraps a Secret A.I. Recruiting Tool That Showed Bias Against Women," CNBC, updated October 11, 2018, https://www.cnbc.com/2018/10/10/amazon-scraps-a-secret-ai-recruiting-tool-that-showed-bias-against-women.html.

62 "The good news . . . can create them.": Joy Buolamwini, "How I'm Fighting Bias in Algorithms," TEDxBeaconStreet, November 2016, https://www.ted.com/talks/joy_buolamwini_how_i_m_fighting_bias_in_algorithms/transcript?subtitle=en.

63 "Thinking about you.": Dina Bass, "Clippy's Back: The Future of Microsoft Is Chatbots," *Bloomberg,* March 30, 2016, https://www.bloomberg.com/features/2016-microsoft-future-ai-chatbots/.

63 "To engage and . . . smarter she gets.": Elle Hunt, "Tay, Microsoft's AI Chatbot, Gets a Crash Course in Racism from Twitter," *Guardian* (US edition), March 24, 2016, https://www.theguardian.com/technology/2016/mar/24/tay-microsofts-ai-chatbot-gets-a-crash-course-in-racism-from-twitter.

67 "The trouble with . . . source of information.": Tatum Hunter, "Chatbots Are So Gullible, They'll Take Directions from Hackers," *Washington Post,* November 2, 2023, https://www.washingtonpost.com/technology/2023/11/02/prompt-injection-ai-chatbot-vulnerability-jailbreak/.

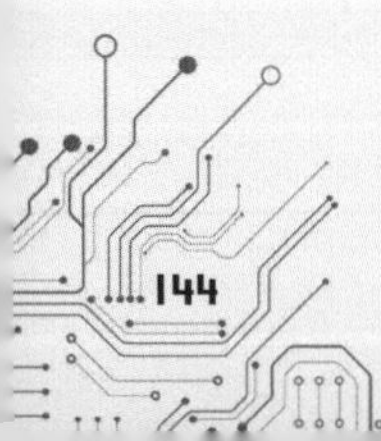

67, 69 “That is why . . . can be fixed.”: Matt O’Brien, Associated Press, “DEF CON to Set Thousands of Hackers Loose on AI,” *Tulsa World,* May 14, 2023, https://tulsaworld.com/news/nation-world/government-politics/def-con-to-set-thousands-of-hackers-loose-on-ai/article_76c6d9e5-b52d-5577-b246-d6249d267f37.html.

68 “You should be . . . problems you encounter.”: “Blueprint for an AI Bill of Rights: Making Automated Systems Work for the American People,” White House, October 2022, https://www.whitehouse.gov/wp-content/uploads/2022/10/Blueprint-for-an-AI-Bill-of-Rights.pdf.

69 “There is such . . . of systemic harms.”: Sarah Kessler and Tiffany Hsu, “When Hackers Descended to Test A.I., They Found Flaws Aplenty,” *New York Times,* April 16, 2023, https://www.nytimes.com/2023/08/16/technology/ai-defcon-hackers.html.

71 “Where humans cannot . . . Jill can automate.”: Kim Bussing, “Georgia Tech’s Teaching Assistant “Jill Watson” Turns Out to Be a Robot!,” *DOGONews,* September 10, 2016, https://www.dogonews.com/2016/9/10/georgia-techs-teaching-assistant-jill-watson-turns-out-to-be-a-robot.

72 “AI has allowed . . . for my patients.”: Lohr, “A.I. May Someday.”

72 “AI and algorithms . . . their work partners.”: Eric Topol, *Deep Medicine: How Artificial Intelligence Can Make Healthcare Human Again* (Hachette, 2019), 18.

73 “Mayo’s role is . . . with these algorithms?”: “The Future of Medicine,” in *Artificial Intelligence: A New Age of Possibilities, Time,* special edition, 2024, 42.

74 “Well, it created . . . was totally wrong.”: “ChatGPT and AI Integration in Health Care with John D. Halamka, MD, MS, AMA Update,” transcript of podcast, AMA, March 13, 2023, https://www.ama-assn.org/practice-management/digital/chatgpt-and-ai-integration-health-care-john-d-halamka-md-ms.

76 “We wanted to . . . has been discovered.”: Anne Trafton, “Artificial Intelligence Yields New Antibiotic,” *MIT News,* February 20, 2020, https://news.mit.edu/2020/artificial-intelligence-identifies-new-antibiotic-0220.

76 “It is the . . . their full potential.”: Mallika Seshadri, “LAUSD Launches Ed, the Nation’s First Personal Assistant for Students,” EdSource, March 20, 2024, https://edsource.org/2024/lausd-launches-ed-the-nations-first-ai-personal-assistant-for-students/708127.

77 “I suspect in . . . a virtual world.”: “Khan Academy Founder Sal Khan on AI and the Future of Education,” *ReThinking with Adam Grant,* TED podcasts, August 15, 2023, https://www.ted.com/podcasts/rethinking-with-adam-grant/khan-academy-founder-sal-khan-on-ai-and-the-future-of-education-transcript.

78 “Amusing but strange”: “*Sunspring*—the Story Told by AI,” Boston Global Forum, December 31, 2018, https://dukakis.org/news-and-events/sunspring-the-story-told-by-ai/.

78–79 "Fantastic win for . . . complementary to humans.": Dani Anguiano and Lois Beckett, "How Hollywood Writers Triumphed over AI—and Why It Matters," *Guardian* (US edition), October 1, 2023, https://www.theguardian.com/culture/2023/oct/01/hollywood-writers-strike-artificial-intelligence.

80 "I think where . . . at the forefront.": "James Cameron on How AI Will Impact Creativity and Innovation," BusinessThink, UNSW, November 6, 2023, https://www.businessthink.unsw.edu.au/articles/james-cameron-ai-creativity-and-innovation.

80 "Underscores the profound . . . AI will have.": "Klarna AI Assistant Handles Two-Thirds of Customer Service Chats in Its First Month," Klarna, February 27, 2024, https://www.klarna.com/international/press/klarna-ai-assistant-handles-two-thirds-of-customer-service-chats-in-its-first-month/.

80 "A great disruptor . . . world of work.": Anna Cooban, "AI Will Shrink Workforces Within Five Years, Say Company Execs," CNN, April 5, 2024, https://www.cnn.com/2024/04/05/business/ai-job-losses/index.html.

81 "At the end . . . or career path.": "1 in 3 Companies Will Replace Employees with AI in 2024," Resume Builder, November 8, 2023, https://www.resumebuilder.com/1-in-3-companies-will-replace-employees-with-ai-in-2024/.

82 "Like the revolutions . . . disrupt labor markets.": Klaus Schwab, "The Fourth Industrial Revolution, What It Means, How to Respond," World Economic Forum, January 14, 2016, https://www.weforum.org/stories/2016/01/the-fourth-industrial-revolution-what-it-means-and-how-to-respond/.

84 "The number of . . . become new jobs.": Matthew Urwin, "AI Taking Over Jobs: What to Know About the Future of Jobs," Built-In, February 23, 2024, https://builtin.com/artificial-intelligence/ai-replacing-jobs-creating-jobs.

84 "Design, development, testing . . . in the workplace.": "Fact Sheet: Biden-Harris Administration Unveils Critical Steps to Protect Workers from Risks of Artificial Intelligence," White House, May 16, 2024, https://www.whitehouse.gov/briefing-room/statements-releases/2024/05/16/fact-sheet-biden-harris-administration-unveils-critical-steps-to-protect-workers-from-risks-of-artificial-intelligence/.

84 "In addition to . . . for all workers.": Rebecca Rainey, "Humans Should Oversee AI at Work, White House Tells Employers," *Bloomberg Law News,* May 16, 2024, https://news.bloomberglaw.com/daily-labor-report/humans-should-oversee-ai-at-work-white-house-tells-employers.

85 "Humanity is on . . . super charge efforts.": "Secretary-General Calls on States to Tackle Climate Change 'Time Bomb' Through New Solidarity Pact, Acceleration Agenda, at Launch of Intergovernmental Panel Report," United Nations, accessed February 23, 2025, https://press.un.org/en/2023/sgsm21730.doc.htm.

87 "The race for . . . good carbon absorbers.": Rob Mitchum, "Researchers Generate a Carbon Capture Breakthrough Using AI, Physics, and Supercomputers," *UIC Today,* February 14, 2024, https://today.uic.edu/researchers-generate-a-carbon-capture-breakthrough-using-ai-physics-and-supercomputers/.

88 "One of the . . . the real world.": Anna Du, "Anna Du: Removing Microplastics from Our Oceans," interview, Wild Planet, accessed February 25, 2025, https://wildplanetfoods.com/blogs/blog/removing-microplastics-from-our-oceans-with-anna-du.

92 "My students and . . . postharvest food losses.": Brad Buck, "From a Small Town in China, Engineer Helps Lead UF/IFAS AI Programs to New Heights," UF FAS, April 10, 2023, https://blogs.ifas.ufl.edu/news/2023/04/10/from-a-small-town-in-china-engineer-helps-lead-uf-ifas-ai-programs-to-new-heights/.

93 "Fundamentally speaking, if . . . to track deforestation.": Christ Stokel-Walker, "TechScape: Turns Out There's Another Problem with AI—Its Environmental Toll," *Guardian* (US edition), August 1, 2024, https://www.theguardian.com/technology/2023/aug/01/techscape-environment-cost-ai-artificial-intelligence.

94 "Everyone thought I . . . to be honest.": Malika Khurana and Hiroko Tabuchi, "Tracking an Invisible Climate Menace from 360 Miles Above," *New York Times,* March 3, 2024, https://www.nytimes.com/interactive/2024/03/03/climate/methane-satellite-launch-global-warming.html.

95 "ChatGPT is not . . . feed a computer.": Sharon Adarlo, "Critics Furious Microsoft Is Training AI by Sucking Up Water During Drought," Futurism, September 26, 2023, https://futurism.com/critics-microsoft-water-train-ai-drought.

96 "Carbon negative, water . . . waste by 2030.": Melanie Nakagawa, "Progress on the Road to 2030," Microsoft on the Issues, blog, February 13, 2025, https://blogs.microsoft.com/on-the-issues/2025/02/13/progress-on-the-road-to-2030/.

99 "A robot may . . . or Second Law.": "Three Laws of Robotics," *Encyclopedia Britannica*, November 23, 2024, https://www.britannica.com/topic/Three-Laws-of-Robotics.

99 "A robot may . . . come to hard.": "Three Laws."

100 "Sounds like a robot to me": "Unimate—the First Industrial Robot," Association for Advancing Automation, accessed June 2, 2024, https://www.automate.org/robotics/engelberger/joseph-engelberger-unimate.

101 "We worked for . . . call it Shakey.": David Szondy, "Fifty Years of Shakey: The 'World's First Electronic Person," *New Atlas*, June 18, 2015, https://newatlas.com/shakey-robot-sri-fiftieth-anniversary/37668/.

101 "The world's first electronic person": Szondy.

102 "It was the . . . perceive its environment.": Elaine Woo, "Charles Rosen, 85: Pioneer in Artificial Intelligence," *New York Times*, December 24, 2002, https://www.latimes.com/archives/la-xpm-2002-dec-24-me-rosen24-story.html.

102–103 "Building from the . . . to complex behavior.": Hansen Hsu, interviewer, "Oral History of Rodney Brooks," *IEEE Annals of the History of Computing,* October/December 2023, https://www.computer.org/csdl/magazine/an/2023/04/10333114/1St7Ega1xe0.

103 “What is this . . . away his career.”: Hsu.

103 “Wow. That’s like . . . walk over everything.”: Hsu.

103 “The most difficult . . . common sense reasoning.”: John Markoff, *Machines of Loving Grace: The Quest for Common Ground Between Humans and Robots* (HarperCollins, 2015), 117.

105 “Our people have . . . do their job.”: Michelle Miller, “Bringing Back Jobs to the U.S. via the Robot,” *CBS Evening News*, October 5, 2023, https://www.cbsnews.com/news/bringing-back-jobs-to-the-us-via-the-robot/.

106 “We have not . . . hands it to me.”: Eric Rosenbaum, “A Robot Named Baxter Wanted to Change the World of Work, but His Career Ended Early,” CNBC, updated September 2, 2022, https://www.cnbc.com/2022/09/01/for-industrial-cobot-its-been-a-decade-in-search-of-a-permanent-job-.html.

106 “So Kismet interacted . . . interact with robots.”: Cynthia Breazeal, “The Rise of Robots,” TED Talk, transcript, February 11, 2011, https://www.ted.com/talks/cynthia_breazeal_the_rise_of_personal_robots/transcript.

107 “I thought, this . . . and empower us.”: Ann Friedman, “Cynthia Breazeal: The Robotics Engineer Whose New Creation Will Bring a Touch of Humanity into Your Home,” *Gentlewoman*, Spring & Summer 2016, https://thegentlewoman.co.uk/library/cynthia-breazeal.

109 “Why was the . . . too many problems.”: Yiannis Kourtoglou, “Hello AInstein! Robot with ChatGPT Shakes Up Cyprus Classrooms,” Reuters, April 4, 2023, https://www.reuters.com/technology/hello-ainstein-robot-with-chatgpt-shakes-up-cyprus-classrooms-2023-04-04/.

109 “It mimics human . . . is getting there.”: Kourtoglou.

110 “Using technology such . . . and accompany them.”: Chengcheng, ed., “Across China: AI Robots Newest Recruits in China’s Kindergartens,” Xinhuanet, July 17, 2018, http://www.xinhuanet.com/english/2018-07/17/c_137330328.htm.

110 “It wasn’t just . . . across the globe.”: “PASCAL International Education Unveils AInstein Junior: Revolutionising Education Through AI Innovation,” PASCAL International Education, February 20, 2024, https://www.pascal.ac.cy/news/news/view/-board/group/post/pascal-international-education-unveils-ainstein-junior-revolutionising-education-through-ai-innovation.

111 “You want robots to . . . movement every time.”: Hessie Jones, “Has AI Robotics Revolution Met Its ChatGPT Moment? A Conversation with Peter Chen, Co-Founder of Covariant,” *Forbes*, August 15, 2023, https://www.forbes.com/sites/hessiejones/2023/08/15/has-ai-robotics-revolution-met-its-chatgpt-moment-a-conversation-with-peter-chen-co-founder-of-covariant/.

112 “You could hope . . . maybe even faster.”: Matt Simon, “The Education of Brett the Robot,” *Wired*, September 21, 2017, https://www.wired.com/story/the-education-of-brett-the-robot/.

113 “These robots are . . . life more fun.”: Malcolm Foster, “Aging Japan: Robots May Have Role in Future of Elder Care,” Reuters, March 27, 2018, https://www.reuters.com/article/technology/aging-japan-robots-may-have-role-in-future-of-elder-care-idUSKBN1H33AB/.

114 "I feel less . . . my best friend.": Jennnifer Yang, "Meet Paro, a Furry Friend to Dementia Patients," *Toronto Star*, October 5, 2015, https://www.thestar.com/news/insight/meet-paro-a-furry-friend-to-dementia-patients/article_27475512-53f2-5d2c-be6b-7e0f4d4e283d.html.

115 "We just don't . . . into the future.": John Leland, "Can Robots Save Nursing Homes?," *New York Times*, April 21, 2022, https://www.nytimes.com/2022/04/21/realestate/nursing-home-robots.html.

117 "Having AI-having that . . . from the planet.": Mike Wall, "Meet CIMON, the 1st Robot with Artificial Intelligence to Fly in Space," Space.com, June 29, 2018, https://www.space.com/41041-artificial-intelligence-cimon-space-exploration.html.

118 "They're kind of . . . of the family.": Eve Herold, *Robots and the People Who Love Them* (St. Martin's, 2023), 162.

118 "The test is inhumane.": Herold, 162.

118 "Ten to fifteen . . . will be robotic.": Riley Ceder, "One-Third of US Military Could Be Robotic by 2039: Milley," *DefenseNews,* July 14, 2024, https://www.defensenews.com/news/2024/07/14/one-third-of-us-military-could-be-robotic-by-2039-milley/.

119 "The urgent need . . . autonomous weapons systems.": "Resolution Adopted by the General Assembly on 22 December 2023," United Nations, February 25, 2025, https://documents.un.org/doc/undoc/gen/n23/431/11/pdf/n2343111.pdf.

120 "The fresh thinking . . . the years since.": Matt Williams, "The Drive for Autonomous Vehicles: The DARPA Grand Challenge," Herox, accessed February 25, 2025, https://www.herox.com/blog/159-the-drive-for-autonomous-vehicles-the-darpa-grand.

122 "America's most challenging . . . get it right.": Ed Shanahan, "How Will Self-Driving Cars Handle Jaywalkers?," *New York Times*, April 2, 2024, https://www.nytimes.com/2024/04/02/nyregion/driverless-cars-new-york.html.

123 "Wanted to showcase . . . the human experience.": Jesus Jiménez, "An A.I. Robot Named Sophia Tells Graduates to Believe in Themselves," *New York Times,* May 15, 2024, https://www.nytimes.com/2024/05/15/nyregion/dyouville-university-commencement-robot-speaker.html.

123 "I offer you . . . and personal growth: Jiménez.

124 "Anything is possible. Go bills.": Jiménez.

124 "I want everyone . . . of my existence.": Mustafa Suleyman with Michael Bhaskar, *The Coming Wave: Technology, Power, and the Twenty-First Century's Greatest Dilemma* (Crown, 2023), 72.

124 "Eight-year-old . . . raising a child." Suleyman, 72.

125 "Consciousness seems pretty . . . up. Watch out.": Kristin Houser, "Sophia the Robot Talks Elon Musk, Climate Change, and More: Freethink Picks the 'Brain' of the World's Most Famous Humanoid," Freethink, January 7, 2023, https://www.freethink.com/robots-ai/sophia-the-robot-interview.

125–126 "An ultra intelligent . . . it under control.": Nick Bostrom, *Superintelligence: Paths, Dangers, Strategies* (Oxford University Press, 2014), 4.

126 "Deliberately inviting aliens . . . they get here.": Matthew Hutson, "Can We Stop Runway A.I?," *New Yorker*, May 16, 2023, https://www.newyorker.com/science/annals-of-artificial-intelligence/can-we-stop-the-singularity.

127 "We're going to . . . in your brain.": Zoë Corbyn, "AI Scientist Ray Kurzweil: 'We Are Going to Expand Intelligence a Millionfold by 2045,'" *Guardian* (US edition), June 29, 2024, https://www.theguardian.com/technology/article/2024/jun/29/ray-kurzweil-google-ai-the-singularity-is-nearer.

127 "Robots the size of a molecule.": Corbyn.

128 "It'll be a pretty fantastic future.": Corbyn.

128 "When people around . . . [threat] for democracy?": Erica L. Green, "Harris Warns That the 'Existential Threats' of A.I. Are Already Here," *New York Times,* November 1, 2023, https://www.nytimes.com/2023/11/01/us/politics/kamala-harris-ai.html.

130 "I'm not here . . . hand-wringing about safety.": J. D. Vance, "Remarks by the Vice President at the Artificial Intelligence Action Summit in Paris, France," The American Presidency Project, February 11, 2025, https://www.presidency.ucsb.edu/documents/remarks-the-vice-president-the-artificial-intelligence-action-summit-paris-france.

130 "Ensuring AI is . . . global dialogue.": Romain Dillet, "As US and UK Refuse to Sign Paris AI Action Summit Statement, Other Countries Commit to Developing 'Open, Inclusive, Ethical' AI," TechCrunch, Febuary 11, 2025, https://techcrunch.com/2025/02/11/as-us-and-uk-refuse-to-sign-ai-action-summit-statement-countries-fail-to-agree-on-the-basics/.

130 "An entirely new . . . the global stage.": Dan Milmo, "Global Disunity, Energy Concerns and the Shadow of Musk: Key Takeaways from the Paris AI Summit," *Guardian* (US edition), February 14, 2025, https://www.theguardian.com/technology/2025/feb/14/global-disunity-energy-concerns-and-the-shadow-of-musk-key-takeaways-from-the-paris-ai-summit.

131 "So a lot . . . underrate the humans.": Greg Rosalsky, "10 Reasons Why AI May Be Overrated," NPR, August 6, 2024, https://www.npr.org/sections/planet-money/2024/08/06/g-s1-15245/10-reasons-why-ai-may-be-overrated-artificial-intelligence.

132 "We need to . . . their rights protected.": Jacy Reese Anthis, "We Need an AI Rights Movement," *Hill*, March 23, 2023, https://thehill.com/opinion/cybersecurity/3914567-we-need-an-ai-rights-movement/.

132 "Nonsensical and non-pragmatic.": "Open Letter to the European Commission Artificial Intelligence and Robotics," Robotics-Openletter.eu, accessed February 25, 2025, https://robotics-openletter.eu/.

132 "Artificial intelligence (AI) . . . in various ways.": Carnegie Mellon University, "Robots and Rights: Confucianism Offers an Alternative," ScienceDaily, May 25, 2023, https://www.sciencedaily.com/releases/2023/05/230525141526.htm.

133 "A different kind . . . be more human.": David Brooks, "Many People Fear A.I. They Shouldn't," *New York Times,* July 31, 2024, https://www.nytimes.com/interactive/2024/07/31/opinion/ai-fears.html.

Selected Bibliography

Baum, Jeremy, and John Villasenor. "How Close Are We to AI That Surpasses Human Intelligence?" Brookings, July 18, 2023. https://www.brookings.edu/articles/how-close-are-we-to-ai-that-surpasses-human-intelligence/.

Baum, Jeremy, and John Villasenor. "The Politics of AI and Political Bias." Brookings, May 8, 2023. https://www.brookings.edu/articles/the-politics-of-ai-chatgpt-and-political-bias/.

Bostrom, Nick. *Superintelligence: Paths, Dangers, Strategies*. Oxford University Press, 2014.

Brumfiel, Geoff. "New Proteins, Better Batteries: Scientists Are Using AI to Speed Up Discoveries." NPR, October 12, 2023. https://www.wliw.org/radio/news/new-proteins-better-batteries-scientists-are-using-ai-to-speed-up-discoveries/.

Buolamwini, Joy. *Unmasking AI: My Mission to Protect What Is Human in a World of Machines*. Random House, 2023.

Captain, Sean. "How AI Can Tackle 5 Global Challenges." Yahoo/Finance, October 29, 2023. https://finance.yahoo.com/news/ai-tackle-5-global-challenges-130006202.html.

Cuellar, Mariano Florentino (Tino). "The UK AI Summit Opened a New Chapter in AI Diplomacy." Carnegie Endowment, November 9, 2023. https://carnegieendowment.org/posts/2023/11/the-uk-ai-safety-summit-opened-a-new-chapter-in-ai-diplomacy?lang=en.

Dodhia, Rahul. *AI for Social Good: Using Artificial Intelligence to Save the World*. John Wiley and Sons, 2024.

Ford, Martin. *Rule of the Robots: How Artificial Intelligence Will Transform Everything*, Basic Books, 2021.

Green, Erica L. "Harris Warns That the 'Existential Threats' of A.I. Are Already Here." *New York Times,* November 1, 2023. https://www.nytimes.com/2023/11/01/us/politics/kamala-harris-ai.html.

Heaven, Will Douglas. "The Education of ChatGPT." *MIT Technology Review,* May/June 2023, 42–47.

Heikkila, Melissa. "The Robots We've Always Wanted." *MIT Technology Review*, May/June 2024, 27–33.

Herold, Eve. *Robots and the People Who Love Them: Holding on to Our Humanity in an Age of Social Robots*. St. Martin's, 2024.

Hill, Kashmir. "Wrongfully Accused by an Algorithm." *New York Times*. Updated August 3, 2020. https://www.nytimes.com/2020/06/24/technology/facial-recognition-arrest.html.

Hutson, Matthew. "Can We Stop Runaway A.I.?" *New Yorker,* May 16, 2023. https://www.newyorker.com/science/annals-of-artificial-intelligence/can-we-stop-the-singularity.

Jackson, Philip C. *Everything You Need to Know About Artificial Intelligence*. A360 Media, 2023.

Jacobs, Sam, editor in chief. *Artificial Intelligence: A New Age of Possibilities. Time* special edition, 2024.

Johnson, Steven, host. "DeepMind's Demis Hassabis on the Future of AI (Transcript)." *TED Interview,* July 28, 2022. https://www.ted.com/podcasts/ted-interview/deepminds-demis-hassabis-on-the-future-of-ai-transcript.

Kissinger, Henry A., Eric Schmidt, and Daniel Huttenlocher. *The Age of AI and Our Human Future.* Little, Brown, 2021.

Lee, Kai-Fu, and Chen Qiufan. *AI 2041: Ten Visions for Our Future.* Currency, 2021.

Levi, Ryan, and Dan Gorenstein. "AI in Medicine Needs to Be Carefully Deployed to Counter Bias—and Not Entrench It." NPR, June 6, 2023. https://www.npr.org/sections/health-shots/2023/06/06/1180314219/artificial-intelligence-racial-bias-health-care.

Li, Fei-Fei. *The Worlds I See: Curiosity, Exploration, and Discovery at the Dawn of AI.* Flatiron Books, 2023.

Lu, Yiwen. "'Lost Time for No Reason': How Driverless Taxis Are Stressing Cities." *New York Times,* November 20, 2023. https://www.nytimes.com/2023/11/20/technology/driverless-taxis-cars-cities.html.

Markoff, John. *Machines of Loving Grace: The Quest for Common Ground Between Humans and Robots.* Ecco, 2015.

Masterson, Victoria. "9 Ways AI Is Helping Tackle Climate Change." World Economic Forum, February 12, 2024. https://www.weforum.org/agenda/2024/02/ai-combat-climate-change/.

Metz, Cade. *Genius Makers: The Mavericks Who Brought AI to Google, Facebook and the World.* Penguin, 2021.

Pelley, Scott. "Is Artificial Intelligence Advancing Too Quickly? What AI Leaders at Google Say." *60 Minutes,* July 9, 2023, transcript. https://www.cbsnews.com/news/google-artificial-intelligence-future-60-minutes-transcript-2023-07-09/.

Roose, Kevin, and Cade Metz. "How to Become an Expert on A.I." *On Tech: A.I. Newsletter.* First of a five-part series. *New York Times,* April 2023. https://www.nytimes.com/article/ai-artificial-intelligence-chatbot.html.

Rothman, Joshua. "Why the Godfather of A.I. Fears What He's Built." *New Yorker*, November 13, 2023. https://www.newyorker.com/magazine/2023/11/20/geoffrey-hinton-profile-ai/.

Shane, Janelle. *You Look like a Thing and I Love You: How Artificial Intelligence Works and Why It's Making the World a Weirder Place.* Little, Brown, 2019.

Smith, Chris. "What Does AGI FOOM Mean, and Should You Worry About ChatGPT Doing It?" *BGR (Boy Genius Report),* November 28, 2023. https://bgr.com/tech/what-does-agi-foom-mean-and-should-you-worry-about-chatgpt-doing-it/.

Suleyman, Mustafa. *The Coming Wave: Technology, Power, and the 21st Century's Greatest Dilemma.* Crown, 2023.

Sun, Tianqi "George." "Is AI Taking Over the Job Market?" *Michigan Journal of Economics,* January 3, 2024. https://sites.lsa.umich.edu/mje/2024/01/03/is-ai-taking-over-the-job-market/.

Topol, Eric. *Deep Medicine: How Artificial Intelligence Can Make Healthcare Human Again.* Hachette, 2019.

Topol, Eric. "Geoffrey Hinton: Large Language Models in Medicine. They Understand and Have Empathy: Perceptions from the Godfather of A.I." *Substack,* December 8, 2023. https://erictopol.substack.com/p/geoffrey-hinton-large-language-models.

Trafton, Anne. "Artificial Intelligence Yields New Antibiotic." *MIT News*, February 20, 2020. https://news.mit.edu/2020/artificial-intelligence-identifies-new-antibiotic-0220.

Vincent, James. "How Much Electricity Does AI Consume?" *Verge,* February 16, 2024. https://www.theverge.com/24066646/ai-electricity-energy-watts-generative-consumption.

Wooldridge, Michael. *A Brief History of Artificial Intelligence: What It Is, Where We Are, and Where We Are Going.* Flatiron Books, 2020.

Young, Jeff. "Why AI Is So Thirsty: Data Centers Use Massive Amounts of Water." *Newsweek*, March 24, 2024. https://www.newsweek.com/why-ai-so-thirsty-data-centers-use-massive-amounts-water-1882374.

Further Information

Books

Achakji, Joseph. *Machine Learning: Fun Ways for Teenagers to Learn About Machine Learning—Dive into AI with Projects You'll Love.* Published by the author, 2023.
This thirty-page book provides a simple explanation of machine learning, discusses ways in which a machine powers games and apps, and encourages creativity in devising your own projects.

Brezina, Corona. *Artificial Intelligence and You.* Rosen Young Adult, 2019.
Brezina covers the many ways that AI is already incorporated into our lives. The benefits and dangers of AI's rapid development are also discussed.

Idzikowski, Lisa, ed. *AI, Robots, and the Future of the Human Race.* Greenhaven, 2019.
This book provides an overview of the benefits and dangers of artificial intelligence.

Lexicon, Leo. *AI for Smart Pre-Teens and Teens Ages 10–19: Using Artificial Intelligence to Learn, Think, and Create. Explore Machine Learning, Deep Learning, LLMs, and the New STEM Opportunities Created by AI.* Published by the author, 2023.
Lexicon discusses the history of AI and ethical concerns and provides insights from experts such as Sam Altman and Andrew Ng on the future of AI.

Schlesinger, Emily. *Artificial Intelligence.* Saddleback, 2024.
This title presents a succinct but high-interest explanation of AI, spotlighting popular examples of AI, such as driverless taxis and robot waiters.

Scientific American editors. *Artificial Intelligence.* Rosen, 2023.
The editors of one of the most respected science magazines provide broad coverage of the history and future of AI, current debates, and ethical concerns surrounding the technology.

Films

The Age of AI. Hosted by Robert Downey Jr. YouTube Originals. Updated April 2020.
A series of nine documentaries covers a wide range of issues relating to AI, including topics such as robots and the job market, medical breakthroughs, and how AI can help solve global problems.

A.I. Artificial Intelligence. Directed by Steven Spielberg. DreamWorks Pictures, Amblin Entertainment, Stanley Kubrick Productions, 2001.
An AI robot with the body and emotions of a child seeks acceptance and love from humans.

Coded Bias. Directed by Shalini Kantayya. PBS. Premiered March 22, 2021.
This documentary highlights the work of computer scientist and activist Joy Buolamwini as well as fellow scientists, mathematicians, and human rights groups as they expose discrimination in algorithms and lobby for accountability and transparency in developing AI.

Enthiran. Directed by S. Shankar. Sun Pictures, 2010.
In *Enthiran* ("robot" in Tamil). a popular Indian movie, a scientist creates a humanoid robot, Chitti, to protect the world. When an evil character inserts a chip to disrupt its program, the robot embarks on destructive behavior.

Machine Learning: Living in the Age of AI. Directed by Chris Cannucciari. Produced by Wired. Supported by McCann Worldgroup, 2019.
Explore ways in which the lives of children, senior citizens, farmers, and others are impacted by AI.

Road to AI. Open Source Stories. Red Hat, 2017.
Part of a Red Hat Films documentary series, this seventeen-minute, award-winning movie explores ways in which AI can be used to make self-driving cars safer.

The Smartest Machine on Earth. PBS, 2011.
An episode on the popular science show *Nova*, this film explores how computers learn to play chess and covers the early history of Watson as researchers attempted to create an AI system that could compete on *Jeopardy*.

2001: A Space Odyssey. Directed by Stanley Kubrick. Metro-Goldwyn-Mayer, 1968.
In this iconic film, the last surviving astronaut on a mission to Jupiter engages in a life-and-death struggle with the ship's sentient and strong-willed computer, HAL.

WALL-E. Directed by Andrew Stanton. Pixar Animation Studios for Walt Disney Pictures, 2008.
A trash-removing robot on a deserted planet Earth falls in love with a more recent, streamlined robot that arrives on a starship.

We Need to Talk About AI. Directed by Leanne Pooley. Produced by Matthew Metcalfe. Spacific Films, 2020.
Experts discuss the existential dangers and the promised benefits of AI as well as how we should prepare for the future.

Websites

STEMpedia: Community Projects by Students
https://ai.thestempedia.com/community-project/
Browse links to a wide variety of AI projects developed by students, teachers, and institutions in the STEMpedia community. These include such systems and devices as a smart weather detector, a personal health companion, and an AI robot for delivering medicine.

UNICEF Innovation: Children and AI
https://www.unicef.org/innovation/sites/unicef.org.innovation/files/2018-11/Children%20%2B%20AI%20Framework_%20Long%20Version.pdf
The site examines the advantages and risks that AI poses for children.

UNICEF: What Is Artificial Intelligence—and How Does It Affect YOU?
https://www.voicesofyouth.org/ai
This Voice of Youth website has a link to a UNICEF international survey on young people's ideas about AI, rights and AI, a section of questions and answers, and links to further knowledge.

Index

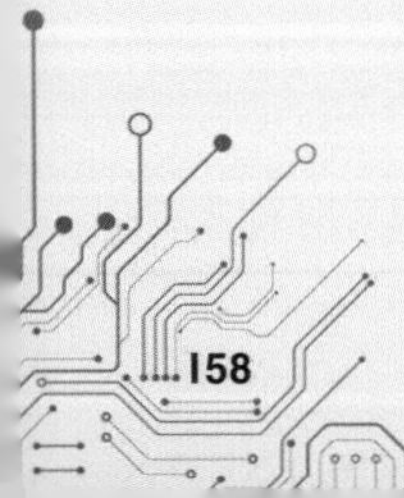

Acknowledgments

The author would like to thank her editors Mariana Montbriand and Lauren Foley for their invaluable comments and suggestions and Richard McPherson for sharing his expertise in the field.

Photo Acknowledgments

Image credits: Johannes Simon/Getty Images, p. 5; API/Gamma-Rapho via Getty Images, p. 6; AP Photo/H. Rumph, Jr., p. 10; CORBIS/Corbis via Getty Images, p. 15; US Army Photo/ARL Technical Library, p. 16; Margaret Minsky, p. 19; AP Photo/Robert Kaiser, p. 20; ShadeDesign/Shutterstock, p. 25; Karjean Levine/ Getty Images, p. 27; David Paul Morris/Bloomberg via Getty Images, p. 31; Pascal Le Segretain/Getty Images, p. 33; AP Photo/Lee Jin-man, p. 38; Google Deepmind, pp. 41, 91; Eleanor Bentall/Corbis via Getty Images, p. 42; AP Photo/Alastair Grant, p. 43; Cosmopolitan, p. 48; Domenico Fornas/Shutterstock, p. 49; Dr Joy Buolamwini (CC by 4.0), p. 58; Suzi Pratt/Getty Images for Refinery29, p. 59; Bill Hinton/Getty Images, p. 66; Thomas Barwick/Getty Images, p. 72; Jay L. Clendenin / Los Angeles Times via Getty Images, p. 79; Bruno Guerreiro/Getty Images, p. 87; David McNew/Getty Images, p. 89; quantic69/Getty Images, p. 95; Aaron Rapoport/ Corbis/Getty Images, p. 99; SRI International (CC BY-SA 3.0), p. 101; Kristoffer Tripplaar/Alamy, p. 105; Rick Friedman/Corbis via Getty Images, p. 107; DIRK WAEM/Belga/Sipa via AP Images, p. 112; Horizons WWP/Alamy, p. 114; Courtesy of Exploring Carolina Canyons expedition via National Oceanic and Atmospheric Administration, p. 116; TANGI QUEMENER/AFP via Getty Images, p. 120; Smith Collection/Gado/Getty Images, p. 122; Imago/Alamy, p. 125; Toby Melville/Pool Photo via AP, p. 129; Zhang Bin/China News Service/VCG via Getty Images, p. 131; Lyu Ming/China News Service/VCG via Getty Images, p. 133. Design elements: Artistdesign.13/Shutterstock; Foryoui3/Shutterstock; Golden Dayz/Shutterstock. Cover: Yuichiro Chino/Getty Images.

About the Author

STEPHANIE SAMMARTINO McPHERSON is a former teacher and freelance writer who has written more than thirty books and numerous magazine stories. Her recent books include *Breakthrough: Katalin Kariko and the mRNA Vaccine* and *Wild Fire: The Culture, Science, and Future of Fire,* coauthored with Ferin Davis Anderson and winner of the 2025 Green Book Earth Award in young adult nonfiction.

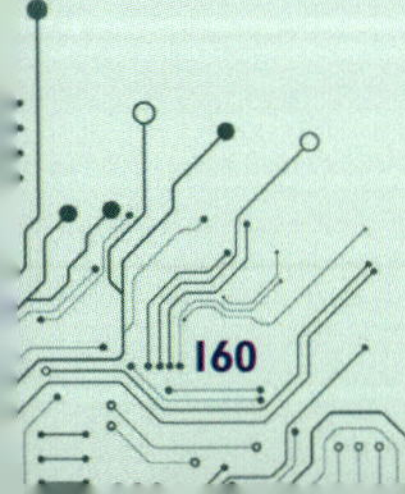